To

DOROTHY WILFORD

Acknowledgement

I AM indebted to the work of C. Stirling Saunder, L.R.C.P. (Lond.), and Henry Gilbert, D.BIO-CH., M.B.S., M.B.B.A., in the field of biochemic treatment, which has made it possible for me to write this book. I have found the work of Professor V. H. Mottram, and Professors McCance and Widdowson, of particular value when studying mineral and vitamin nutrition, and in applying the principles of sound nutrition to promoting good health. I have also to thank the Editors of *Here's Health* for permission to include here some part of my article dealing with assimilable iron in foods, which was first published in their pages.

HOW TO USE THE
TWELVE TISSUE SALTS

By
ESTHER CHAPMAN
L.S.N.T., A.B.B.A.

A guide to the biochemic treatment
of pain and disease

THORSONS PUBLISHERS LIMITED
37-38 Margaret Street, London, W.1

First published 1960
Reprinted March 1964
Reprinted January 1968
Reprinted July 1970

12-87

*This book has been set in Baskerville, printed in Great Britain
on Antique Wove paper by Anchor Press,
Tiptree, Essex*

ISBN O 7225 0112 9

Contents

Foreword

THE prescriptions given inaugurate the necessary
remedial effects within the body: they adjust
mineral defects, which was shown by Paracelsus
and others after him to be the cause of many
conditions of disease.

Introduction

THE food we eat, produced by vegetable and animal life, consists of material which has been absorbed by the plant or animal into the fibres of its own organism from simpler forms of chemical life. The plant takes up the minerals in the soil and the carbon in the atmosphere from which it embodies its own substance, and the animal, and fish, eat plant and other forms of living organisms for their structural maintenance.

Human beings use this organic food in combination with the air they breathe and the water they drink for the various purposes needed by their physical tissues. The process of digestion and the correct assimilation of that food is one of breaking down much of that organized material into its simpler constituents, amino-acids, sugar, mineral elements, carbon, hydrogen, oxygen, and their absorption by the body tissues. Where this operation proceeds normally throughout all its tissues, the body is in health. The ceaseless activity of this complicated process constitutes the body's metabolism.

Various diseases and injuries disrupt, increase, or lower a person's metabolism.

The cells of the human body are composed of inorganic and organic material: the intake of air, food and drink has to provide these constituents.

The health of the physical tissues is also affected by the person's individuality, by the hopes, despair, by the faith or fears which dominate the mentality. In physical terms it is not possible to say of what hope and faith consist, but we have all seen these qualities inspiring human beings and their physical effects on the body are not to be denied. The eye becomes brighter, the cheeks improve in colour, and vigour is some degrees increased: obviously a chemical change has affected the blood to good purpose, and in all healing this is a salient factor of great value.

11

1

The Nutrient Remedies

THE biochemic nutrient-remedies, which embrace also the Schussler tissue salts, are inorganic mineral substances, the very same of which our earth and its soils are composed. When these are suitably selected and prepared and taken as remedies for various diseases or physical disturbances, a food substance is being taken in a simpler form than the meals normally contain, thus requiring no break-down of a complicated substance. This is a great advantage where the various links of the digestive processes are weak or functionless. Disease invariably brings a disturbance of metabolism: shrunken, weak, or thickened conditions of cell life with function disrupted, or the metabolism may be heightened and displaced as in fevers, injuries and inflammations.

Biochemic tissue remedies provide an immediate answer for both serious and slight disturbances, which when correctly diagnosed and treated should only require one other factor for success, the life-energy of the person taking this treatment.

Originally, the analysis of the blood and tissues of a healthy human being, and of its maternal milk, revealed the presence of twelve inorganic salts. Subsequent analysis has added many more such substances, but in microscopic amounts and they have become known as "trace" elements: even so they are essential to the life of the organism. Some of these apparently act as co-ordinators, others as activators of secondary chemical processes within the body.

All the substances of earth, sand, and rock, weathered and washed down into the springs and rivers, and many of the contents of the sea are carried in infinitesimally small amounts into the tissue life of human beings through heredity and the food they eat. The microscopic amounts of these substances may be no more than a small part of an atom.

The eminent German physiological chemist, Bunge, has given this analysis of the blood:[1]

In every 1,000 grammes of blood-cells—

Iron (Phosphate)	0·998 grammes	
Potassium Sulphate	0·132	,,
Potassium Chloride	3·079	,,
Potassium Phosphate	2·343	,,
Sodium Phosphate	0·633	,,
Calcium Phosphate	0·094	,,
Magnesium Phosphate	0·060	,,

And in 1,000 grammes of the intercellular fluid—

Sodium Chloride   5·545 grammes

And with even smaller amounts of other salts.

Any unbalance of these salts and any disturbance of metabolism causing disease has therefore to be considered as extremely small, and the needed dosage of a biochemic nutrient to meet the condition has to be reckoned accordingly in microscopic amounts. This is achieved by the trituration process in the preparation of these nutrient remedies.

These tissue salts in their natural state consist of closely packed particles of the elements and are thus not assimilable by the cell tissues. They are therefore "triturated", which is a crushing and spreading-out process, by which the particles of the salt are spread over a large area and mixed with pure sugar of milk, a convenient neutral medium in itself. The result is an attenuation of the particle of the salt according to the number of times of "spread" and mixing.

[1] Ref.: *Guide to Biochemic Treatment*, by C. Stirling Saunder, l.r.c.p.(Lond.).

The salts are prepared for medication in the 3x potency,[1] 6x potency, and 12x potency, and higher potencies of 30x and 200x are obtainable: they are also procurable in the mixed range of 3x–200x for each tissue salt. This is a combination of the various potencies scientifically prepared by high-powered machines in order to achieve a subdivision of the particles of the salt which will correspond most closely with its counterpart in the living tissues.

It is best to give doses of the smallest suitable strength. By this means other functions of the cells proceeding normally will not be disturbed or unbalanced. In chronic conditions of disease, however, several functions of cell life are likely to become involved and those several conditions will then need attention and given suitable treatment. The higher the trituration, the more divided and the finer is the substance. The condition of some tissue cells requires a very fine or high trituration before the weakened cell tissue can absorb it. Some conditions may also require certain nutrients in quantity amounts, and the food intake then needs adjustment and possibly some food supplements.

These mineral elements, being a part of the nutrition of the body, support the food intake; the food has to supply the body's organic needs.

As constituents of its cell life and intercellular processes, these mineral elements are a factor in effective elimination of waste and worn-out cell products, and in the dispersal of congestions harmful to the health of the body.

The cells of body tissues have the power to attract the substances from the blood needed for their nutriment: in ill-health this power may be weakened and consequently a high (fine) trituration of the remedy would be needed.

It is difficult to make an exact alignment when considering the mineral elements contained in food and the potency triturations of the prepared mineral remedies. Those contained in our food have mostly become compounds in forming the structures of cereals, vegetables, fruit, flesh food and dairy

[1] And are now obtainable in any potency from 1x upwards.

produce, and the digestive process is the simplification of these structures into assimilable factors. In comparison, the preparation of the inorganic mineral substances as biochemic tissue remedies is one of division into minute assimilable portions of an element.

In particular, brain and nerve cells attract as their related cell-salts Kali. Phos., Mag. Phos., Nat. Phos., and Ferr. Phos.: similarly muscle cells, with the addition of Kali. Mur. Connective and lining cells, by which the tissues are covered and connected with other body tissues and are also protected and given strength, especially attract and require Silicea; elastic tissue, which will include cartilage and again the muscle cells, Calc. Fluor. The cells of mucous membranes attract Nat. Mur. Bone-tissue has affinity for Calc. Fluor., Calc. Phos., and Mag. Phos.; the skin attracts Kali. Sulph., and Silicea; the hair cells also. Ferr. Phos. is needed by every cell of the body.

In addition, all conditions of first-stage inflammations – raised temperature, soreness of throat, rash – will require Ferr. Phos. to assist the extra demand on the blood cells for haemoglobin and oxygen.

In chronic disease the most obvious symptom indicates the first requirement; the secondary and the general condition of the patient will most probably need a supporting prescription for the constitutional unbalance, or the basic tissue remedy may need supporting trace elements. Suitable doses of biochemic tissue remedies can provide all these requirements of the tissue cells and intercellular tissue.

The number of cellules constituting the dose is shown by the laboratory, or the practitioner supplying these mineral remedies.

Age is bound to be a factor in the recovery from illness or injury and from disease: it has been said that where a child takes a week to reinstate its health, an elderly person will need four or five times as long. But one does not need to wait for full recovery to enjoy a measure of relief and greater ease.

The therapeutic section outlines the treatments to be

followed in various conditions of pain and disease, having the broad principles of cause and effect in mind. It has to be remembered, also, when diagnosing the condition, that it is the person, or child, we wish to heal and not merely the symptom. Thus, a child with chronic eczema may first need a tonic for the pituitary gland or the nervous system before the skin condition will respond to the tissue remedies Kali. Sulph., Ferr. Phos., and Kali. Mur. Consequently, this child and some of the chronic sufferers may need more experienced biochemic treatment than is contained within these Twelve Salts. Reference to these special requirements is also given in the therapeutic treatments. In short, diagnosis to be successful needs often to be intuitive as well as having the necessary physiological knowledge.

II

The Twelve Inorganic Tissue Salts

	Therapeutic name
Fluoride of Lime (Calcarea fluorica)	Calc. Fluor.
Phosphate of Lime (Calcarea phosphorica)	Calc. Phos.
Sulphate of Lime (Calcarea sulphurica)	Calc. Sulph.
Phosphate of Iron (Ferrum phosphoricum)	Ferr. Phos.
Chloride of Potash (Kali. muriaticum)	Kali. Mur.
Phosphate oi Potash (Kali. phosphoricum)	Kali. Phos.
Sulphate of Potash (Kali. sulphuricum)	Kali. Sulph.
Phosphate of Magnesia (Magnesia phosphorica)	Mag. Phos.
Chloride of Soda (Natrum muriaticum)	Nat. Mur.
Phosphate of Soda (Natrum phosphoricum)	Nat. Phos.
Sulphate of Soda (Natrum sulphuricum)	Nat. Sulph.
Silicic Acid (Silicea)	Silicea.

III

The separate functions of the Twelve Tissue Salts in the healthy human body: and the potency and dose needed in pain and disease

So fundamental, so essentially necessary are the Tissue Salts in daily life that there follows a detailed description of each, and its uses, each under its special heading. Also shown are the *diseases and pain* resulting from an unbalance or deficiency of these Tissue Salts in the human body and suggested *doses and potencies* to be taken for relief and the restoration of health.

Fluoride of Lime (Calc. Fluor.)

This salt is a constituent of all the connective tissues of the body. These tissue cells cover all organs, and form unbroken connexions between the various tissues and organs. Connective tissues run through all muscles, support the blood vessel walls, and form part of the skin of the body. The covering tissue of the bones contains this salt, and it forms the enamel of teeth.

Where there is an unbalance of this salt in the connective tissues, organs are likely to become prolapsed and veins varicose. Flabbiness, generally, shown in the flesh and in a hanging abdomen indicates a disturbance in the correct assimilation of this mineral from the food. This may similarly affect the heart muscle, which then suffers from dilatation. And the answer is to give a higher (finer) potency of the mineral to effect permeability of the tissue cells and so ensure correct assimilation.

Rough and sensitive teeth indicate a poor distribution in the body of this mineral, or an actual deficiency, and it is probably the reason for a late dentition in an infant.

If muscle tendons suffer a strain, or if they lose firm shape and form a tumour, or lymphatic glands become enlarged, if carbuncles form, or hard ulcers in the primary state before any inflammation or suppuration has commenced, these are indications of an unbalance in the particles of this mineral salt which require the use of suitable doses of Calc. Fluor. as a remedy. And if the skin runs into cuts and cracks with a crust forming, this condition, too, indicates a need for Calc. Fluor.

Some cases of gastric vomiting probably require Calc. Fluor. for an unbalance of this mineral localized in the gastric connective tissue. If, however, the vomit is greenish, Nat. Sulph. will be needed, or Nat. Phos., if the vomit if frothy and sour-smelling. (See reference to these two salts.) Again, where the urine is pungent, this may be caused by a similar localized disturbance, and if the urine has passed testing or is an apparently healthy elimination, doses of Calc. Fluor. should give the right condition.

For ruptures, haemorrhoids, and haemorrhage of the uterus, again because of a local weakness of the connective walls, take doses of this remedy. These conditions will most likely require a combination of several tissue salts in alternation, e.g. if bleeding haemorrhoids are the condition, Ferr. Phos. will be needed in addition, but if the bleeding is clotted, Kali. Mur. will be needed in alternation with Calc. Fluor. In weakness of the throat where the larynx is relaxed, Calc. Fluor. is again the indicated tissue salt, in alternation with, most probably, Kali. Mur.

Chronic conditions of synovitis need Calc. Fluor. to correct the unbalance in the affected tissues, as also any swellings of the covering of bones.

Doses of this tissue salt are a remedy for obesity in alternation with doses of Calc. Phos. to adjust poor assimilation of starches and fats in the meals. At the same time, the intake of these foods will advisedly need to be checked over.

When using this tissue salt for acute conditions, give Calc. Fluor. in a 6x potency, and if the symptoms are severe, a dose every ten or fifteen minutes is indicated. As soon as the condition is easier, the doses should be taken less frequently and then at two-hourly or three-hourly intervals. Chronic conditions generally do better if higher potencies are used. Should a chronic condition flare up, then a high potency of the salt taken at half-hourly intervals will be needed for a short time. As soon as there is an abatement, the doses can be given only four times a day, or even once a day if the case is an advanced one or the patient is an elderly person.

Very young children are best given a half-dose every ten minutes in acute conditions.

If the combination potency 3–200x is used, it is equally suitable for acute and chronic conditions, additional frequency only being needed for acute conditions.

Phosphate of Lime (Calc. Phos.)

Farmers and gardeners know this salt. It is a main constituent of many of the productive soils.

This salt is also a main constituent of all the cells of the body and the body fluids. It has an attraction for albumen, in combination with which it builds new cells for the blood; it is an important element of the gastric juice, and of all bone and teeth.

This tissue salt promotes growth in children: doses of the 6x potency are indicated in any defective development and to effect restoration in wasting diseases. Similarly, it is of great value in rickets in combination with specific foods and vitamins.

Calc. Phos. can be used with advantage in all cases of debility, and in convalescence, for tuberculous conditions, and particularly where there is poor assimilation of food and consequent defective nutrition.

In cases where discharges have lowered and exhausted the

system, this remedy should follow doses of Calc. Sulph. which will have arrested them.

If broken bones do not unite or are slow to do so, or the fontanelles in children remain open, use Calc. Phos. as a remedy.

This salt is needed as a remedy in conditions of the blood and circulation which result in cramp, or spasm with numbness (not to be confused with spasm of the nerves with shooting pains which needs a different tissue remedy, Mag. Phos.). If hands and feet are always cold, or if the hands and feet are ice-like and clammy, or if the circulation is slow or retarded, making parts of the body feel as if they were asleep, Calc. Phos. is the indicated remedy.

Where albumen is exuded, Calc. Phos. is the remedy to adjust the disturbance.

This remedy is needed in diphtheria if the larynx is involved, and in croup (in alternation with Kali. Sulph. to hasten the expulsion of dead cell material).

Calc. Phos. should be used in a high potency by those who catch cold easily, and who are much subject to catarrh: one dose a day should generally be sufficient to cure this liability. In these cases it may be necessary to adjust the balance of the general diet.

Doses of this salt are indicated for spinal curvatures, polypus, and for deep ulcers; also, for neuralgias which have numbness.

If there is a tendency to form "stones" of phosphates – the diagnosis may be given as calculi – doses of a high potency of this salt should correct the mineral unbalance present in this condition, and should be used from time to time to prevent a recurrence.

Some cases of obesity need this remedy in conjunction with Calc. Fluor., and possibly some small adjustment in the food intake, particularly as to the consumption of starch.

Conditions of hydrocele, orchitis, sore breasts in women, and chronic ovaritis, are also indications of a disturbance or deficiency of phosphate of lime, and Calc. Phos. is the indicated tissue salt: the general food habits may also need supplementing.

Night sweats indicate a disturbance of metabolism which this remedy is likely to adjust; and some cases of epilepsy will be helped by doses of this tissue salt.

In cases of considerable flatulence, if doses of Mag. Phos. (in hot water) are insufficient to cure the condition, follow up the dose of Mag. Phos. with a dose of Calc. Phos., and repeat this procedure after each meal, or at stated intervals while the attack persists.

When giving this remedy for gastric trouble, as a restorative after debilitating diseases, and usually when there is anaemia, cellules of Nat. Mur. may need to be given also to assist assimilation of calcium. (See Nat. Mur.)

All conditions needing this nutrient remedy can be given the 6x potency (or the 3–200x) except tumours, which will require a higher potency: the 12x (or the 3–200x) is advised as likely to be effective.

Sulphate of Lime (Calc. Sulph.)

This salt is known on the commercial market as plaster of Paris, and its surgical use is as plaster casts for the support of fractured limbs.

In the human body it is a constituent, in the form of minute particles, of all connective tissue, and is contained also in the cells of the liver.

This salt in the physical tissues attracts water to itself, and in that way hastens the destruction of certain worn-out cells. In the liver, its presence there effects the destruction of the red blood cells which have finished their cycle of life and have arrived at the liver as partially waste products. If, then, there are insufficient particles of Calc. Sulph. in the liver the blood becomes over-charged with these worn-out cells and skin eruptions generally result.

If the deficiency of the particles of this salt extends to the connective tissues, the skin eruptions are likely to become deep abscesses or chronically oozing ulcers. Where varicose ulcers have become chronic and sanious – causing much lowering and draining of the system, these are indications for the use of Calc. Sulph. as a remedy. Again, if the face is covered with pimples and pustules which continue to suppurate, Calc. Sulph. is the tissue remedy.

This remedy is used for third-stage inflammations (these give exudations of pus), particularly where wateriness of the tissues is also present: the pus itself may be watery, as in some conditions of bronchitis.

This nutrient-remedy can be useful after doses of Nat. Sulph. in kidney diseases.

Frontal headaches with sickness are probably due to a general deficiency of particles of Calc. Sulph. in the connective tissues of the nerves; if the *elderly* have neuralgia this may be from the same cause; and where there is extreme touchiness of the nerves and much sensitiveness, these are indications for taking Calc. Sulph. to remedy the condition.

Suggested doses: for a chronic condition – a dose of 6x, or of 3–200x, three times a day; for elderly people – a dose of 12x, or of 3–200x, three times a day, but if the condition is of long standing this dose only twice a day; for young people – give a dose of 6x, or 3–200x, four times or even six times a day where the condition is probably more of an acute nature.

Phosphate of Iron (*Ferr. Phos.*)

Iron is contained not only in the blood cells but in all the cells of the body, except those of nerves. These, however, are lined with protective connective tissue, containing blood (with its iron), which penetrates between the cells and nourishes them: phosphate of iron is found in hair cells, and in the muscular membranes of the blood and lymph vessels.

The haemoglobin of the blood is composed of iron in combination with the protein, globin. Its presence in the tissues is the means by which carbon dioxide in those tissues is given off and returned to the lungs. Iron in association with Kali. Sulph. carries oxygen to all tissues of the body. The presence of iron in the tissues also activates various processes in the body, including that of releasing energy from the food that has been digested.

The red corpuscles in the blood have their cycle of life, comprising from two to six weeks, and on their disintegration the iron from them is stored in the liver until it is used again. Healthy kidneys hold back much of the iron that would be otherwise lost in the urine, though some part of the body's iron content is lost in the process of sloughing of skin, perspiration, and in faeces elimination.

Copper is an essential element in catalysing (activating) the manufacture of haemoglobin in the body. Thus, the body not only requires iron, but also the trace element, copper, to co-operate with it.

The body only absorbs iron when it requires it, but it is one of the first requirements for health and adequate supplies should be present in the daily food. Iron that is not wanted and has not been absorbed from the food is duly excreted in faeces waste.

Insufficient hydrochloric acid in the digestive juices may prevent the absorption of iron even from those foods which contain it in an easily assimilable form. This can be a reason for an iron deficiency in the blood even though the intake of suitable food may be adequate.

If there is an unbalance in the particles of iron in the fibres of blood vessels, these become relaxed and congested. If, then, such a condition does not adjust itself, inflammation of various tissues results. Most physical illness commences in this manner, and if used promptly, doses of this nutrient will most probably heal the condition. If, however, a further stage of inflammation has been reached (second- and third-stage inflammation), giving exudations and secretions, it is well then to use doses of this tissue remedy in alternation with that indicated by the type of exudation.

One cause of continuous diarrhoea is the relaxed walls of the intestinal *glands*: a cause of constipation is a weak bowel action consequent upon relaxed muscular walls of the *intestines*.

In both conditions it is probable that insufficient iron is being absorbed from the food, either from inadequate supplies or from too little hydrochloric acid in the digestive juices. In both these cases doses of this tissue salt can be expected to bring the condition to normal if they are also alternated with similar doses of Nat. Mur. in a little water to correct the digestive juices. If costive, the stools are dry, which is an indication of the trouble, and the remedy. The daily meals should, of course, be checked to see that adequate supplies of *assimilable* iron are, in fact, being taken.

Minimal doses of this tissue salt will correct functional disturbances, and can be given for congestion and haemorrhage due to an accumulation of blood. Congestive headaches probably need this remedy (with, in addition, doses of Kali. Sulph.), as also some cases of insomnia from lack of iron nutrition to the brain. If, after some hours of concentrated brainwork in the late evening, sleep is elusive, a dose of this remedy followed ten minutes later by a similar dose of Kali. Phos. can be expected to clear the brain and natural sleep should follow shortly after.

This remedy can be used for nose-bleeding, and is indicated in uterine haemorrhage and where the menses are excessive.

Ferr. Phos. has great value as a remedy for all recent physical injuries to assist healing of the parts in supplying the needed additional iron particles. Doses should be taken internally at ten-minute intervals, and externally as a lotion with a bandage by dissolving some three doses in half a cupful of warm water.

The severe pain from inflamed piles is quickly relieved with this remedy: use it also if they are bleeding. In these cases a dose every ten minutes is advised until the most acute condition has lessened, when every hour, and then two-hourly intervals are suggested. The condition can be treated externally as well, using a lotion of this tissue salt, some three doses to half a cupful of warm water.

This tissue salt is also an excellent general remedy for

children, in alternation with Calc. Phos., and particularly if they are listless, have no appetite, or have teething fever. A 12x potency of the Ferr. Phos., and a 6x potency of the Calc. Phos. is suggested, or both in the 3–200x potency: three doses of each daily until recovery, which will generally be accomplished in twenty-four hours.

Ferr. Phos. is specially to be recommended as a remedy in the first stages of any illness or disease, to enable the blood the better to fight the illness by an attempt to increase its qualitative power. This tissue remedy should be used at the commencement of all colds, sore throats, and influenzas, for the first stages of all fevers, for all children's fevers – scarlet fever, whooping-cough, measles – for the first stage and also during the illness, and for similar conditions in adults; also for the first stages of bronchitis, pleurisy, and rheumatism, and as one of the remedies in neuritis at the commencement of pain.

The simplest indications for the use of this tissue remedy are a raising of temperature, the head is hot, with internal shivering, brilliant and inflamed eyes, and if any part of the body is obviously hot and inflamed, or if the throat is sore.

For all first stages of an illness, on immediate injury, and for suddenly inflamed or bleeding piles, a 6x potency is likely to be suitable, or that of the 3–200x. If the trouble is *highly* acute, take a dose every ten minutes, but half-hourly doses would generally be considered suitable for acute conditions, and then hourly and less frequently as the condition eases.

Many illnesses advance to a second-stage inflammation, either because they have not been observed and dealt with in time or the patient's general constitution has allowed an inroad of the disease to a further stage. The use of Ferr. Phos. as a remedy will always assist in breaking down the disease and in fortifying the life of the body. Where the condition has advanced to second- and third-stage inflammations, the indicated tissue remedies for those conditions should first be given and the Ferr. Phos. given also as a second or third requirement, and less frequently than the then main remedy.

In very debilitated or elderly people the higher potencies of Ferr. Phos. are likely to be most suitable for all treatment, and a 12x, 30x, or even 200x potency can be used. These can be taken for acute and for chronic conditions: doses might well be taken hourly for acute conditions, and twice or three times a day where the trouble is more of a chronic nature.

For most adults, unless in a weak state of health, the 3x potency is suitable for most acute conditions, and a 12x potency would probably be required if the trouble had become chronic over a period of time.

The 3–200x potency can be expected to cover most requirements, the frequency of the dose being the only adjustment for the acute and chronic conditions, and the slower metabolism of the elderly needing one or two doses a day for long-standing conditions.

Chloride of Potash (Kali. Mur.)

Potassium Chloride has an attraction in the body for fibrin – a nitrogenous protein.

If there is tissue irritation under the surface cells of the skin, these cells increase their natural activity of excreting cell substances and the skin is raised into a blister. In the body Kali. Mur. unites with hydrogen and forms hydrochloric acid: this then dissolves the excretion. This happens in smallpox and in chickenpox, in scarlet fever, and measles, and Kali. Mur. is indicated as a remedy when the activity of excretion has commenced, that is, after the fever has begun to abate. In the first stage of fever Ferr. Phos. is needed. (See page 27.)

The lining cells of all body tissues form a thin covering membrane. These secrete sufficient fluid to nourish the adjacent tissues and keep them moist. If these membranes suffer inflammation, similarly, the secreting activity of these cells will increase. The secretions will at first be watery and copious, and need Nat. Mur. as a remedy. If the inflammation has extended to a second stage, Kali. Mur. is needed and suitable doses will dissolve the fibrinous element in these secretions: they are generally recognized as a greyish-white catarrh. Doses of Kali. Mur. will clear this catarrh by adjusting the secreting activity.

Eczema will be resolved by this remedy if it is in the secondary stage of inflammation, that is if the skin is blistering and commencing to excrete, but all pathological skin conditions are invariably much helped with the addition also of Kali. Sulph.

Croupous conditions, pneumonia, and pleurisy, indicate a need for this remedy.

This secondary inflammation is present in mumps, with consequent swelling of the glands, and in some cases of deafness where the eustachian tubes have become swollen and congested, and doses of this tissue remedy can be expected to clear it. Some cases of catarrhal deafness are of long standing, and this chronic condition will need a high potency to be effective.

For retinal exudation and granulation of the eyelids, and where there is dry granular inflammation from the nose, Kali. Mur. is the indicated tissue remedy: if the menses are painful and membranous – bringing away shreds of thin, dead tissue, use this tissue salt in alternation with Mag. Phos. If the menses blood is dark and clotted, this is a certain indication for the need of this tissue salt, as well as for the condition of leucorrhoea, the whitish exudation from the vagina.

Kali. Mur. in suitable potencies is indicated where the liver is sluggish, with constipation giving only light, greyish stools; for piles with dark clotted blood; and for rheumatic fever after the high temperature has abated, and for which the Ferr. Phos. would be needed.

For typhoid, enteric, and typhus fevers, this remedy is indicated, *with Kali. Phos.*

Again, Kali. Mur. is indicated in mucous colitis: the earlier stage of inflammation and pain has required Ferr. Phos.

Warts on the hands are healed with this tissue remedy, and it is indicated for healing shingles, and for acne.

If given immediately, the 3x potency as a lotion will control the blistering in burns and scalds. (Ferr. Phos. will be needed in alternation and should relieve the pain.)

Dull, aching pains in any part of the body need this remedy: the condition is generally to be treated as an acute one, needing the 3x potency (or the 3–200x potency), a dose every twenty minutes.

If starch and fatty foods are taken with difficulty, this is most probably due to a deficiency of Kali. Mur. in the saliva, where it is an aid to the effective digestion of starch, and one dose each morning in the 6x potency is advised as a constitutional remedy.

This tissue salt is also indicated for jaundice when the condition is due to a chill, because of catarrh of the duodenum being present, and for asthma when this is due to gastric disorder, as the condition requires Kali. Mur. to assist secretion of hydrochloric acid: for this reason it is an important remedy in epilepsy. Disease of the heart, liver, or kidneys, *with dropsy*, may be expected to require suitable doses of this salt.

In all acute conditions the 6x potency of this tissue salt can be expected to give the correct results, taken internally, a dose every twenty minutes: where it is needed externally as a lotion, the 3x potency is preferable. In chronic conditions of sluggishness of the liver with constipation, a 12x potency is advised, a dose three times a day.

The 3–200x potency is suitable for all cases: a dose every twenty minutes for acute conditions, and three times a day where the condition has become a chronic one.

Some three doses in half a cupful of water makes a suitable lotion, applied on lint.

Sulphate of Potash (Kali. Sulph.)

This tissue salt has a special relationship for those cells forming the lining of the skin and those which form the internal mucous lining of all the organs of the body.

If the balance of this salt is disturbed in these tissues, there is a disruption in these lining cells and an exudation of yellowish slimy matter is the result. Papules of the skin secreting this type of exudation, usually with irritation, indicate this unbalance in the surface cells; and a yellow coating at the back of the tongue is a symptom of this condition involving the inner membrane of the digestive tract.

This tissue salt shares with Ferr. Phos. in the activity of carrying oxygen to all tissues of the body, and which has first been taken up by the iron in the blood cells.

Kali. Sulph. in conjunction with the oxygen in the body activates the destruction of its worn-out cells, and at the same time it prevents undue dissolution. It is a third-stage inflammation tissue remedy, needed for its action in normalizing such processes.

Kali. Sulph., then, is the tissue remedy in third-stage inflammatory conditions of bronchitis, whooping cough, penumonia, when the exudations are of this yellowish, slimy nature; and in *all* catarrhs having this type of exudation, whichever part of the body is involved – in gastric, intestinal, laryngeal, nasal, or aural catarrhs; and in all those diseases when peeling conditions of the skin are in process.

By reason of its relationship with oxygen in the physical tissues, this is the tissue salt to be used in all those conditions – whether it be asthma, rheumatism, or gastric fever – which are worse in hot rooms and in hot atmospheres, or when the fever rises appreciably at night and is near normal in the mornings.

Where there is an insufficiency of particles of this tissue salt, the physical tissues suffer from a need of oxygen. This is experienced in alternate hot and cold feelings, in weariness and heaviness, in vague feelings of anxiety or sadness, in heavy headaches, or in pains in the limbs which are of an indefinite nature and tend to move about, and in rheumatism or neuralgia where these pains move about from part to part of the body. These symptoms worsen in the evenings and are relieved by cool, fresh air.

Kali. Sulph. will be indicated in asthma when the condition is accentuated by being in warm rooms or during hot weather.

This remedy is needed in conditions of peritonitis having the tympanitic abdomen; in jaundice, if the tongue has a yellowish coating – implying a third-stage catarrh as its causation; and in colic if this is catarrhal and has not responded to treatment with Mag. Phos.

Indigestion which gives a feeling of fullness at the base of the stomach may also be catarrhal, in which case the tongue will almost certainly show it, but the condition indicates an insufficiency of the particles of this salt needed for effective oxidation in the tissues involved.

All third-stage inflammations producing tissue degenerations of the surface cells of the mouth, the tongue, the lips, indicate a need for this tissue salt, and any part of the skin or the internal membranes affected in this manner – in psoriasis, eczema in its third stage, and in dandruff: nasal obstructions with ulceration, and foetid discharges of the ear indicate a similar involvement.

All these catarrhal conditions, the bronchitis, the jaundice, and the established skin conditions are likely to be of a chronic nature and treatment with a 6x potency (or the 3–200x potency), a dose three times a day, should quickly improve the condition. A similar potency and number of doses is likely to be correct for conditions of dandruff, and a lotion of some three doses of the 3x potency in half a cup of warm water should be additionally effective. Vaginal discharges having the yellowish exudation are a chronic condition, catarrhal in nature, and doses of the 6x (or the 3–200x) potency three times a day should quickly effect healing, provided other health measures are adequate.

Heavy headaches, indigestion, neuralgia, feelings of alternately shivering and suffocation, and if the menses are difficult or even absent, these conditions even when recurring are of a transitory nature and are treated as for acute conditions. A dose of the 3x potency (or the 3–200x) is correct in these cases, given frequently, every ten minutes, every twenty minutes, and then hourly if further treatment is required. As soon as relief is felt, showing the tissues are reacting to the tissue remedy, the doses should be taken less and less frequently. This is a certain rule for acute conditions. In chronic conditions when there is an *alteration* in the symptoms presented, showing a partial clearance of the trouble, a change of tissue remedy is indicated.

Potassium Phosphate (*Kali. Phos.*)

Potassium Phosphate is an important mineral element in the structure of nerve and brain tissue, of muscles, and of blood cells. It is, in fact, found in all tissues of the body, is antiseptic in character and counteracts decay in the organism, giving the physical tissues vitality.

Kali. Phos. is an essential element in the processes of metabolism, and in the assimilation of digested fats: it is also essential for the process of effectual respiration within the tissues.

In all putrefactive conditions within the body, this tissue salt is needed as a remedy. It is indicated in appendicitis due to a putrefactive bowel, and is the chief remedy in septic conditions, in offensive secretions and diarrhoeas, in septic haemorrhages, and in gangrene.

Kali. Phos. is the chief remedy for typhoid and typhus fevers, and in enteric fever: in these conditions similar alternating doses of Kali. Mur. are needed to support the Kali. Phos. being taken. In stomatitis, and in albumenuria – due to faulty metabolism – Kali. Phos. is again the suitable tissue salt.

Suitable doses of Kali. Phos. are indicated where the brain is in a disturbed condition, resulting in suspicious moods, poor memory, despair, anxiety, fear, tearfulness. Where there is a disturbance of this salt in the motor nerves, this is shown in weakness of nerve response and corresponding weak muscle

B

action, and in paralysis, or in nerve pains with the sensation of paralysis. In all these conditions Kali. Phos. is the tissue nutrient to use.

This tissue remedy is indicated particularly for all pathological excited states, as in hysteria, melancholia, and for obsessional fears; also for sleep walking: it is given for concussion of the brain, and in delirium: for loss of mental power, and for prostration after great exertion resulting in muscular atrophy or producing spasms and cramps: and for impotence, and incontinence.

It is the tissue remedy for sleeplessness when this is due to excitement or brain fatigue from additional stimulation, either from pleasure or overwork.[1] Where the insomnia becomes chronic, the Kali. Phos. doses will almost certainly need the addition of the relative trace elements, all in suitable potencies. These are obtainable.

A small and frequent pulse may indicate a need for Kali. Phos. if this is due to any degeneration of nerve supply.

This tissue salt is needed for alopecia, for nettle-rash, and for malignant pemphigus; for asthma if this is purely nervous; and for nervous palpitation, when the 200x potency is advised.

Kali. Phos. is indicated to reduce fever and pulse if Ferr. Phos. has failed.

Where the menses are excessive, this tissue salt is needed in alternation with Ferr. Phos., and it is also given for colic. Sciatica and neuritis indicate a need for this remedy in alternation with Ferr. Phos.

If children become acutely fretful, Kali. Phos. is needed in alternation with Nat. Phos.

The fevers will need to be treated as acute conditions to commence with: as soon as good reactions have been established and the condition shows an improvement, the doses at twenty-minute intervals will then be given much less frequently, and in alternation with a second or third remedy indicated by the stage of the disease.

[1] The taking of too much salt can be a cause of sleeplessness: indigestion is another.

If the putrefactive or septic conditions are not accompanied by *fever* they will probably need to be treated as of a chronic nature and a dose three times a day is likely to be most suitable. The minimal dose may be difficult to give but it can be extraordinarily effective if correctly prescribed. This is not really surprising when one remembers how delicately poised are chemical balances and how a disturbance in the nature of the particles requires only the minimal for competent absorption.

Diseases of the spinal nerves and of the motor nerves bringing difficulty in the use of muscles and control of function are likely to be of a highly chronic nature, the disease having established itself some time before it has been diagnosed. These conditions need biochemic prescriptions incorporating trace elements in addition to the Kali. Phos., without which this tissue salt is not likely to be fully operative. (Sufferers with these conditions are likely to benefit from *gentle*, experienced massage and directed exercises, depending on the extent of the condition. These measures increase the nutrition of all the tissues and assist the circulation to carry away its retrograde fluids. Their daily meals need to provide them with sufficient vitamins.)

Alopecia, nettle-rash, malignant pemphigus, and nervous asthma, once established, will require treating as chronic conditions, and given three doses daily of Kali. Phos. in a 200x, or preferably, the 3–200x potency.*

All conditions which suddenly present themselves and appear to need this tissue remedy may be judged as acute, but on continuation of the condition the nature of the trouble will have to be regarded as a chronic one and doses given only three or four times a day.

Phosphate of Magnesia (*Mag. Phos.*)

This mineral salt is another element of the blood cells, bones and teeth, of the brain and nerves, and of the muscle cells. If its molecules are out of balance in these tissues, cramp

---

* Chronic skin diseases and asthma will most probably need certain trace elements in the prescription to effect a balance of metabolism,

and spasms result, and if this condition runs to inflammation, neuralgia or even paralysis may result.

Mag. Phos. is the chief tissue salt in effecting functional activity of the motor nerves. This tissue salt is therefore indicated in those pains which are sharp or shooting, or constrictive, or giving spasm, whether they bring headaches, ear-ache, toothache, or rheumatism.

It is the indicated tissue remedy in tetanus, and in lock-jaw (other than conditions of dislocation), for the functional cramp of writers and artists, in nervous asthma, for palpitation of the heart if this is spasmodic, and for angina; also for yawning or shivering if this is spasmodic. The indications for this tissue remedy are the spasms and the shooting pains: those for Kali. Phos. are weakness and the inability to make a movement.

Mag. Phos. is needed in constrictive spasm of the vagina, in painful retention of urine with spasm: for all pains of a colic nature – to soothe teething infants and for their colic pains – and for flatulence.

If there is continued vomiting accompanied by nausea; in whooping cough for the continued "whoop" stage; if there is continued hiccough; and for squinting; for St. Vitus' Dance; and in paralysis agitans; give Mag. Phos. as the needed tissue remedy.

Neuralgias of the face or the stomach or the bowels need this remedy; also menstrual colic and ovarian neuralgia, painful membraneous menstruation – in alternation with doses of Kali. Mur. – conditions of spasm of the glottis, quinsy, the stabbing pains of goitre, and for hypertrophy of the prostate gland. Should there be childbirth convulsions, Mag. Phos. is the needed tissue remedy.

Doses of this tissue salt are indicated for phosphatic sediment in the urine; if there is itching over the whole body; for profuse perspirations; and for brain exhaustion with insomnia, if this is accompanied with spasms.

Many of these pains are eased by *firm* pressure and if the sufferer is given *warmth*.

Those who constitutionally appear to need this tissue salt as a remedy are the highly sensitive and nervous type of person, often thin and easily exhausted, and when in pain sweat considerably.

In treating conditions of colic, convulsions, and cramp, a 6x potency is generally suitable, and frequent doses in a little HOT water are advised. In all other conditions needing this tissue salt a 3x potency is considered more suitable. In most cases, except those of established disability in paralysis agitans, St. Vitus' Dance, squinting, and the glandular diseases of goitre, prostate hypertrophy, and the menstrual cycle, the condition will need to be treated as an acute one and frequent doses of this tissue salt taken in HOT water, since warmth gives additional efficacy. In dealing with these troubles with the 3–200x potency, however, large doses of ten to fifteen cellules will generally give better results.

Chronic conditions of disability, seen in a continuing paralysis agitans, will be likely to need a 30x potency, or even 200x, or the 3–200x potency can be tried: one dose a day is suggested. These doses will probably need supporting trace elements in the prescription.

Chloride of Soda (Nat. Mur.)

This mineral comprises the common salt of everyday use. It has a close affinity for water, dissolving in its watery solution the otherwise insoluble phosphate of lime (Calc. Phos.), and regulating the amount of moisture in the body in its distribution throughout the tissues and intercellular spaces. It is a carrier of moisture to all cells: this is a requirement for cell growth and renewal.

Cells which do not contain this mineral are unable to attract water to themselves and waterlogging in the intercellular spaces results (hydraemia), and is seen in conditions of bloatedness, with watery eyes, or undue salivation. Many of these individuals crave salt.

Common salt is one of the first needs of animals and human beings, all other mineral constituents of the body, as cell foods, being dependent upon it for the process of their distribution and absorption.

The particles of sodium chloride are split up in the peptic glands, and the sodium unites with carbonic acid (set free during the process of metabolism), entering the blood as sodium carbonate. The dissolved chlorine becomes hydrochloric acid, now a constituent of the gastric juice required for dissolving food; dyspepsia is a result of deficient hydrochloric acid.

The serving of common salt to those with hydraemia, or with dyspepsia, does not supply the tissues with the needed remedy. Shrunken tissues, depleted of moisture and this mineral, require this salt in a finely triturated form so that the sick tissues may be able to absorb it. Only the trituration process enables them to do this with the minimum of time and effort. A chronic unbalance is not easily adjusted by diet, but the assimilation of food is greatly assisted with two or three doses of this nutrient.

Where there is an unbalance of this salt in the mucous membranes following chills, fevers, and in the early stage of catarrhs, all conditions showing watery, transparent secretions, Nat. Mur. is the remedy to restore correct function.

This unbalance is apparent in running colds and the watery type of influenza, in hay fever, and in all fevers where there is watery vomit, in excessive lachrymation, in dropsy, in oedema of the scrotum, and in asthma when there is oedema. The same indication is seen in mumps when there is much salivation, in watery blebs or pimples on any part of the body. This remedy is indicated in hydrocele, in epilepsy if the attack is accompanied by frothing, and in pleurisy if this gives watery exudation.

All diseases with watery, acrid, excoriating discharges need doses of this tissue salt. It is indicated in chronic facial eczema, in nettle-rash (with Kali. Phos.), in Addison's disease for the skin condition, and in exophthalmic goitre.

If chronic constipation is of a dry nature, doses of this tissue salt will quickly ease and cure the condition: other conditions of constipation need the appropriate tissue salt and very probably a higher vitamin intake.

This tissue remedy is needed if individuals are habitually chilly with cold extremities – from taking too much salt in the food. When there is numbness of hands and feet, in sterility, and in confinement when the mother's milk is watery and salty, doses of this salt are required.

In cases of sunstroke, for ulcers of the gums, for emaciation if the individual is at the same time well fed, for greasy skins, in pregnancy if the size of the breasts is excessive, for cracked finger-tips, and for neuralgia of the bowel (with Mag. Phos.), Nat. Mur. is the indicated tissue remedy.

If sciatica has not cleared with doses of Kali. Phos. and Ferr. Phos., there may be a constitutional need for this remedy, and it should be given in cases of hysteria, for stupor in illness, and for excessive heaviness of sleep or insomnia.[1]

Insect stings which give watery exudations indicate the need for this remedy, and where there is persistent falling out of the hair with much dryness of the scalp. All conditions where there is too much dryness or too much wateriness, showing an unbalance in the condition of natural moisture, indicate the need for this tissue remedy.

If the pulse is rapid and intermittent, and palpitation is present, or for the feeling of a constricted heart with fluttering, doses of this salt can be expected to bring the condition to normal.

With the exception of cold in the head, the sudden onset of hay fever, and that of collapse after exhaustion, which can be expected to respond to a 6x potency, all other conditions needing this remedy are likely to require a 12x or the 3–200x potency. For the acute condition of sunstroke give a dose of the 12x or 3–200x potency every fifteen minutes.

Catarrhal fevers, mumps with salivation, and dyspepsia, indicate a second-stage inflammation, requiring a semi-acute treatment, and a 12x potency is advised. For watery ulceration of the gums, for watery vomit, for frothy tongue, and for

[1] Less salt food is usually desirable.

dry constipation, these conditions of the digestive tract all indicate the use of a high potency, and the 3–200x is advised. Delirium, excessive heaviness of sleep, and palpitations, also need a high potency in giving doses, and much salivation with dribbling may require the 200x.

All conditions requiring this tissue remedy are likely to respond well to the 3–200x potency.

Phosphate of Soda (Nat. Phos.)

The action of this salt in the body is to decompose lactic acid, which, when not so catalysed, irritates the tissues and causes much suffering in rheumatic subjects. In splitting the lactic acid into carbonic acid and water, the presence of this salt keeps the carbonic acid in the blood until it reaches the lungs, when it is given off on the out-breath.

The action of this salt in the tissues prevents the thickening of bile in the gall duct, assisting the assimilation of fats, and preventing those conditions of jaundice and biliousness due to a bile deficiency.

This salt emulsifies, and is the indicated remedy where fatty acids in the food disagree.

Nat. Phos. also keeps the normal uric acid soluble in the blood. If this tissue salt is out of balance, the uric acid combines with the soda that may be present and is deposited in the joints, producing the inflammation of rheumatism.

When there is acute rheumatism in the joints, or there is gout, the tissue salt, then, is indicated, and in some conditions of arthritis this is one of the remedies needed. (See also Silicea.)

Conditions of nausea will need this remedy and if some underlying nervousness is present, Kali. Phos. should also be used. (These two salts are excellent remedies for travelling sickness.) Where the nausea is of a bilious character, however, the tissue remedy should be Nat. Sulph. (See Nat. Sulph. and the relationship between these two salts.)

Because of the lactic acid condition present, this tissue remedy is needed for sick headaches, especially if these are focused on top of the head, and where there is sour breath and sour vomits, where there is the acid or the coppery taste. This remedy is indicated where there is an offensive odour in front of the nose, and here the tissue salt Mag. Phos. is also needed.

Where there is heartburn, and also where there is pain after food which goes through to the back, for flatulent risings which taste sour, and for acidity which causes diarrhoea or frequent urination which is generally slight; for constipation if acid symptoms are present; for sterility if acidity symptoms are also present; for sour-smelling, creamy leucorrhoea, for honey-coloured secretions of eyes, and in eczema or pemphigus having these secretions: these conditions need suitable doses of this tissue salt.

Catarrhs of thick yellow mucous – a second-stage inflammation – need this remedy: if these are less thick but yellow and slimy, Kali. Sulph. is needed. Diabetic conditions indicate the need for this remedy, together with the use of doses of Nat. Sulph.

Where sleeplessness is accompanied by much itching, and for the acid conditions of little children where there has been too much milk and sugar in the feeding, Nat. Phos. is the tissue remedy.

Where there are inflammations of a phlegmonous type (white leg), with swelling, owing to a breakdown in the activity of the white blood corpuscles, Nat. Phos. is the correct tissue remedy, but it needs to be taken promptly.

These conditions are mostly of an acute character and almost all can be expected to respond to a low potency of 3x. This will be suitable for vomiting from acidity, acute conditions of rheumatism, acidity of stomach, itching, ulceration of gums. If the conditions have persisted and there is continuing sleeplessness from acidity, continuing nausea, continuing sour sweats, a 6x potency is advised.

The 3–200x potency is applicable in all these conditions.

Sulphate of Soda (Nat. Sulph.)
Sulphate of soda appears as a pharmaceutical product in

Glauber's salt. It is slightly irritant to the physical tissues and is used to stimulate natural secretions.

This salt in particle form is a constituent of the intercellular fluids of the body. Its function is to eliminate superfluous water from the system, including decomposition products of lactic acid, which have been brought about by the action of Nat. Phos. (See Nat. Phos.)

Nat. Mur. has an affinity for water and carries moisture to the tissue cells: Nat. Sulph. has a similar attraction, but for that moisture which has become a product of retrograde processes, and which it draws to itself for elimination purposes. These two salts promote the balance in absorption and elimination of water necessary for the continuing life cycle of the cell tissues.

Nat. Sulph. has a stimulating effect on the lining cells and also on the nerves of the bile ducts, the intestines, and the pancreas. It is consequently the remedy for biliousness, for some types of constipation and flatulence, and becomes a nerve remedy in the relationship between the spleen, the pancreas, and the solar plexus. It has a stimulating action on the "filtering" tubes of the urinary system in passing off unwanted water as urine. It increases the secretion of pancreatic fluid, and is of considerable importance as a remedy in conditions of diabetes. (See also Nat. Phos.)

Low fevers indicate a need for this tissue remedy.

Where the leucocytes remain too long in the blood before disintegrating, with resulting leucaemia, this tissue remedy withdraws their moisture and promotes the desired disintegration. The condition indicates an insufficiency of the particles of Nat. Sulph.

Hydraemia may be occasioned by an unbalance of this salt in the intercellular spaces: this condition is shown in oedema of the tissues.

Catarrhs with yellowish-green, or green secretions, bilious fevers, bilious influenza, and bilious vomiting with diarrhoea; bilious irritability with depression and despair, influenza with gripping pain, hydrocele, and dropsy from liver conditions; if the liver is tender from congestion, for kidney and gall-bladder disorders, in jaundice, and in rheumatic conditions suffered by hydraemic patients; these conditions indicate a need for this tissue remedy. All discharges of watery pus, particularly from chronic conditions; soft warts and crops of warts around any part of the body; whitlows; these are also conditions which need doses of Nat. Sulph.

This remedy should be used in bronchial asthma, and in night attacks of asthma; in agglutination of the eyelids, and if there is a flat, soapy taste in the mouth; also, where there is retention and incontinence of urine.

Vomiting in pregnancy may need this remedy if Nat. Phos. and Kali. Phos. in alternation have not proved efficacious, and where there is too much milk in lactation.

This tissue remedy will most probably be needed in phlegmasia alba-dolens with doses of Nat. Phos. (see Nat. Phos.), and in some conditions of constipation, particularly if this seems to be occasioned by a slimy catarrh.

If there is a feeling of burning in the nose, in the mouth, or of the gums; if there is ear-ache with noises in the ears, Nat. Sulph. is the tissue remedy to use.

If the tongue is coated greenish or dirty brown, needing Nat. Sulph. the condition should be considered as acute, and the 3x potency should quickly clear it. The same potency is able to deal satisfactorily with the acute conditions of bilious colic, acute gout, acute sciatica and bronchial asthma if these individuals have hydraemic constitutions. Take frequent doses, half-hourly, or every fifteen to twenty minutes, until the condition is easier, and then much less frequently until the trouble has cleared.

Conditions of nausea, vertigo, bilious or neuralgic sick headaches, excessive sleepiness, noises in the ear, soft warts, soft swellings, these conditions require doses of 6x potency, taken internally: difficult and persisting cases will need higher potencies. Lotions of a 3x potency should be applied concurrently for soft warts and for the soft swellings of erysipelas (with much soft bandaging).

Concussions from injuries may need a second remedy of Nat. Sulph. and a 6x potency is suggested (first remedy, give Ferr. Phos., 3x potency).

In all these conditions doses of the 3–200x potency are applicable.

THE RELATIONSHIP BETWEEN CHLORIDE OF SODA, PHOSPHATE OF SODA, AND SULPHATE OF SODA (NAT. MUR., NAT. PHOS., AND NAT. SULPH.)

Some of the indications for Nat. Mur. as a remedy will also appear to require Nat. Sulph. These salts are closely associated in their actions within the body. Nat. Mur. has the power of attracting moisture to the cells and the intercellular spaces and of regulating the amount there: Nat. Sulph. withdraws retrograde and superfluous moisture. The symptoms of "wateriness" however are heavier and thicker in texture, or of a slimy nature (being retrograde), when the requirement is for Nat. Sulph.

When nausea presents itself as the chief symptom of illness, we have to decide whether the needed mineral nutrient is Nat. Phos. or Nat. Sulph. Because of its emulsifying action, Nat. Phos. is the remedy when fatty foods disagree or there is excess lactic acid.

Some conditions of nausea and sickness are precipitated by the purely nervous factor: in these cases Kali. Phos. needs to be taken as well as doses of Nat. Phos.

Nat. Sulph. is given where biliousness is caused by the decomposition of lactic acid not having been eliminated from the system. Nat. Sulph. is not, strictly speaking, a cell salt, but it is a constituent of the intercellular fluids. It attracts superfluous water in the system to itself and is the factor which causes elimination of the fluid. The superfluous water is a decomposition product. The action of Nat. Sulph. in the intercellular fluids follows that of Nat. Phos. in the tissue cells.

Silicic Acid (Silicea)

Silicic acid is a constituent of all the connective tissue cells of the body, of the hair, the nails, and the skin. This connective tissue covers the brain, the spinal cord, and nerve fibres, and when there is an unbalance of silicea in these tissues, swelling and inflammation result, with pain. The effect of these disturbances, however, may be absorbed through the lymphatics[1] or suppuration may ensue before it is resolved. Suitable doses of silicea will promote the essential absorption.

A deficiency of silicea in the connective tissues causes a lack of an essential nutrient of the brain and nerves, resulting in poor memory, slow and difficult thought, absent-mindedness. Silicea is contained in the epidermis of wheat and other cereals and the eating of whole-grain products in the dietary should provide the normal need for this element.

This tissue salt is able to dissolve the urate of soda (the "poisons") deposited in so many arthritic joints. The capacity for the absorption is determined by the condition of the lymphatics: most of these vessels have valves to assist in the return of lymph and waste products from the tissues to the veins, and their function of good drainage and absorption reflects the health of these tissues.

If uric acid is present in the urine, this tissue salt should be taken in small doses until the trouble disappears.

Indications for the need of silicea are dry feet with an offensive odour, showing a lack of natural perspiration; night-sweats, particularly of the head, and any condition of over-perspiration of feet, arm-pits, with much odour. Doses of silicea should restore the condition to one of normal perspiration without noticeable odour.

All conditions of poor nourishment and weakness, with general irritability – caused by defective assimilation of food – indicate a need for this nutrient remedy. General debility indicates a need for this tissue salt, in combination with Calc. Phos.

Silicea promotes suppuration: boils, carbuncles indicate a

[1] An intermediate vessel between blood and tissues.

need for this tissue salt. It is generally *contra-indicated* in appendicitis, and in torpor of nerves.

Those who tire easily, physically, who are sensitive to much internal chilliness, who have little body heat, those whose menses is accompanied with icy coldness and probably constipation, who easily get headaches from study, nervous exhaustion, or digestive conditions, these are all indications for doses of this tissue nutrient.

If the hair falls out, for conditions of cataract, because of the connective tissues involved, and for some conditions of deafness, this tissue nutrient is the correct remedy.

Where there is ulceration of the nasal bones with discharge, ulceration of the mouth, of the tongue, acrid leucorrhoea, chronic cystitis, thickening of mucous membranes generally with blockage, rheumatic and arthritic concretions, these third-stage inflammations indicate a need for silicea.

This tissue salt has been called the surgeon of biochemistry. It clears foul discharges, foetid diarrhoea, and excretions. It is used for encysted tumours, hard gatherings with pain, anchylosis. Occupational diseases of stone-workers and coal-miners where the dust gets into the bronchi and lungs, need this "surgical" tissue remedy. All irritating, difficult coughs, where there is much trouble in clearing the expectoration, indicate the need for this remedy.

Brittle nails, ribbed, ingrowing nails need this salt.

Obstinate neuralgia, piles giving *much* pain, soreness or tenderness of feet giving lameness,[1] irritation of the spine, bruised or diseased bones; chronic synovitis, chronic conditions of weak ankles, chronic sleeplessness from congestion of blood; these persisting conditions are likely to require this nutrient remedy.

Spasm of sphincter ani, with partial expulsion and receding of stool; stricture of the lachrymal ducts; these conditions need suitable doses of silicea.

---

[1] If lameness is caused by maladjustment of the bones of the feet, experienced manipulative treatment should be sought for possible correction and re-nourishment of the joints and tissues.

All elderly people have a general need for silicea.

The more deep-rooted conditions of ulcerations, diseased bone, inflammation of the breasts, chronic rheumatism and arthritis, tumours, will need doses of silicea in the comparatively high potency of 12x. All other conditions needing this tissue remedy can be expected to clear with the 6x potency. The 3-200x potency is applicable in all cases: two or three doses a day are generally suitable. Any specially difficult condition might well require experienced attendance.

IV

The importance of Food Balance in the daily meals: Table of some comparative Food Values

THE importance of having properly balanced meals cannot be sufficiently stressed. This not only refers to the protein, carbohydrate, and fat content, but to the equally essential mineral and vitamin factors as well.

Individual requirements as to the quantity of food eaten vary widely, according to age, physical condition, occupational needs, personal tastes, and the whole attitude towards the question of feeding oneself. This last is generally a matter of habit or of the emotions. Many people are conservative in food and tend to follow the pattern given them by their parents. Emotional reactions, often unconscious, frequently govern the choice of food, on how much is sufficient, and on its association and attraction values when, and how it comes to table.

When a meal is not properly balanced in its content, some part of its nutritive value is lost. Too much of certain foods may be taken, and too little eaten of certain essential foods to ensure the proper assimilation of the whole. Thus, starch in order to be properly digested needs its complement of vitamin B_1, otherwise the end product, glucose, will be incompletely oxidized, in which case toxins accumulate in the blood and poison the nerves. The choice of whole-grain foods in a meal provides the carbohydrate content and the vitamin B_1, since this vitamin is contained within the outer skins of the grain. There is a similar reason for cooking potatoes in their skins and so retaining most of that vegetable's mineral salts. The natural salts and vitamin factors contained in vegetables and fruits are *essential* to the health of the human body.

The body requires protein to supply its nitrogen needs. The nitrogen obtained from its protein intake has to equal the loss of nitrogen excreted daily in the process of wear and tear of the body's tissues. The protein intake has also to supply essential constituents for the body's metabolic changes, and for building new tissue. Proteins contain approximately sixteen per cent of nitrogen. Some contain much less, but a mixture of protein foods will invariably supply the average needs for nitrogen.

The process of metabolism requires protein, but this activity cannot proceed correctly without the presence of carbohydrates. When carbohydrates are not taken at the same meal, the protein break-down in the liver is burnt to sugars and the body's protein needs for tissue repair and tissue building are not met. If more protein than the body needs is taken at one time, the excess balance is wasted in liver sugar and the body may suffer a protein deficiency later in the day. Though predominantly of one structure or another, most foods contain some amounts of protein, carbohydrate, fat, some minerals and vitamins, all in close association.

Foods assist one another in the process of body metabolism and a mixed diet best keeps the metabolism in balance. Too much protein, and particularly too much animal protein, quickens the rate of metabolism. This is likely to advance the ageing of a life. Too little protein and rather too much carbohydrate and fats is likely to occasion obesity from too little combusion of this material and its consequent deposit in the tissues.

Scientific research and experiments appear to show that I gramme of protein per kilogram of body weight is needed daily. This means that $2\frac{1}{2}$ oz. of actual protein is needed daily by a man weighing 11 st., and 2 oz. of actual protein is needed daily by a woman of 8 st. 12 lb. But the British Medical Association and the Conference of the Food and Agricultural Organization in 1944 recommended that these figures should be raised a little to probably 3½ oz. for a man weighing 11 st. and to 3 oz. for a woman of 8 st. 12 lb. These are *actual protein* figures and *not* the weight of foods containing protein.

The quality of the protein is a further factor of importance, and dairy foods, classed as animal protein, are more wholely broken down and assimilated by the human tissues than are purely vegetable proteins. From the health point of view it is well to observe that the end products of *flesh* proteins occasion putrefaction in the human bowel, and those from starch and vegetable foods give rise to fermentation, providing very obvious reasons for daily evacuations, which should be natural and adequate.

Experiments have shown that the greatest biological value is obtained if half the protein food eaten is from vegetable and half from animal sources; that the amount of actual flesh foods eaten should be limited; and in all cases that it should be offset with fresh vegetables and fruit to give adequate mineral and vitamin content.

Carbohydrates and fats consist of carbon, hydrogen, and oxygen, and are energy foods. They are needed to burn (break down) the proteins to obtain nitrogen release and convert it to the body's needs and are a necessary link in the process of metabolism. Carbohydrates, too, are essential in the structure of body tissues. If carbohydrates and fats are eaten in excess of the body's requirements, they are stored in the tissues. Fats are not properly converted into energy unless sufficient carbohydrates are also eaten. Carbohydrates give bulk to a diet: fats give a greater feeling of satiation.

Nutritionists have believed that a high fat intake has some relationship with the incidence of coronary and vascular diseases, and the investigations carried out by the American,

Dr. Ancel Keys, appear to show conclusively that this is so.

It is considered that a high cholesterol level in the blood is the causative factor in the degeneration of the arteries and an excessive fat deposition in the liver. Cholesterol is a sterol found in combination with fatty acids: foods which have a good cholesterol content are eggs, liver, kidney, and fats (including cream). It is generally inadvisable to eat much of these foods unless there is exceptionally good oxidation,[1] and particularly so of the fats.

Carbohydrates eaten at the same meal aid oxidation of fats, and other factors of metabolism assist in this process: exercise is a factor in the conversion of fat compounds and the accompanying carbohydrates into energy, but not necessarily the cholesterol factor in the fats.

Cholesterol is a constituent of the blood, of the covering of nerve fibres, of the sebum of skin glands, of the bile, and it is found in all the cells and body fluids. In the blood and in the skin glands it has protective value. In some circumstances it crystallizes out and forms gall-stones from too great a concentration in the gall-bladder.

Dr. Keys also found from the studies carried out that "a low fat intake and low values for cholesterol in the blood go together". Fat stimulates the liver to make cholesterol. It was also found that "fats from meat and dairy products are the highest promoters of sebum cholesterol: fish oils and some vegetable oils promote the cholesterol level". Maize oil apparently does not.

Sunshine, and the use of ultra-violet lamps, have the effect of changing the cholesterol into vitamin D within the body. Vitamin D is an essential factor in the absorption of the body's calcium, and promotes the cycle of metabolism. (See also vitamin D values and sources of this vitamin in food: page 76.) This process, however, should not be allowed to become exhaustive, since the body has both its cholesterol as well as

[1] The capacity to take up and combine with oxygen – an essential part of the process of nutrition.

its vitamin D requirements. Sunshine, or the use of an ultra-violet lamp can be expected to lower a too high cholesterol content in the body. It is, also, relatively easy to lower the fat intake (and the cholesterol level) by omitting cream from the diet and controlling the butter and animal fat intake.

The following food balance is suggested:

Protein *foods*:	4–6 oz. daily, depending on the foods chosen, and individual needs.
Carbohydrate *foods*:	Probably 8 oz. or more, daily. This is difficult to determine: more will be needed if a high protein intake is usual, in order to metabolize the protein successfully.
Fats:	8 oz. butter (or other fat and oil) per week.
Fruits and vegetables:	8 oz. or more, daily; and an orange and a tomato are recommended each day.
Additional:	1 pint of milk daily is generally considered advisable, taken in tea, coffee, or used in combination with other food, or taken, itself, as a drink.

Protein foods from animal sources include fresh and dried milk, the various cheeses, eggs, fish, fowl, and meat. The vegetable proteins are the several kinds of nuts, soya flour, whole-grain cereals and pulse foods.

The carbohydrate foods which, in addition to their starch or sugar content, largely retain the vitamins and mineral elements natural to their organism, are the wholemeal or high-extract flours for bread, biscuits and cakes; oats; unpolished rice; dried fruits; honey; black treacle, and the Barbados sugar or "pieces" sugar; potatoes when cooked in their skins and except when they have become "old" potatoes at the end of their season and have lost their vitamin C content; and the pulse foods.

Pulse foods consist of a high concentration of carbohydrate and a lesser concentration of protein: this occurs also in fresh peas, since these are all seeds.

Most fruits and vegetables are predominantly mineral and vitamin foods, except those that more particularly have value for their starch and protein content, namely the peas, beans, potatoes, and root vegetables.

Full-cream milk, cheese, and nuts, contain high percentages of fat, as well as their protein content, and the liberal use of these foods in the dietary generally obviates the need for a higher butter allowance than that shown at 8 oz. a week.

All foods are complex in structure and if not unduly processed retain various proportions of carbohydrates, protein, minerals, and vitamins, natural to their structure. Black treacle, for instance, consists of $28 \cdot 5$ per cent water, $67 \cdot 2$ per cent sugar, $0 \cdot 19$ per cent nitrogen, $1 \cdot 2$ per cent protein, and high contents of the minerals sodium, potassium, calcium, magnesium, iron, copper, phosphorus, sulphur, and chlorine. The amount used with food is very small, but it is taken primarily for its mineral and sugar content, the mineral factor being of value for the blood and the bowels.

In considering any tables of values for the various foods, the actual amount eaten has to be remembered and how often a particular food is acceptable in the daily meals. Nuts give a higher protein value than peas, beans, and the pulses – and with considerably less carbohydrate proportion – but a less amount of nuts is generally eaten (and not all the protein is well digested), which factors occasion a bit of fine judgement as to the ultimate actual protein balance obtained from these different foods.

The value of a meal, as well as the pleasures of the palate, depend on how the different foods are mixed and the amounts taken. Potatoes and nuts served at the same meal to supply the protein and carbohydrate food provide only second-class protein and low vitamin content; also, the mineral content would be somewhat inadequate since we have to remember that the calcium in the nuts is only partly assimilable; and such a dish would give little flavour for the palate. The phytates in the nuts would be offset if watercress or a green vegetable were included, and this would raise the mineral and vitamin content to a more satisfactory level.

Simple though it may be, a poached egg on buttered brown toast, with watercress, or bread and butter and a firm cheese and some well-chosen fruit give a better-balanced meal in every respect. The egg, the cheese, provide the animal or first-class protein, and the bread gives vegetable protein and the necessary balance of carbohydrates: the essential mineral and vitamin content, in addition to that supplied by the egg, the cheese, bread and butter, is augmented by the watercress or the fruit, which might well be an orange or a tomato.

The energy of the universe is convertible. Plants use light from the sun to make proteins, starches and sugars, thus converting energy into their tissues. Man and animals eat these plants and in the process of digestion the energies of the plants are liberated and converted by the process of metabolism into the type of energy that we need.

The taking of a breath needs energy: the flow of blood round the body to all the tissues needs energy in the ceaseless action of the heart muscle. It takes energy to slough off old skin and make new tissues. All external work, too, needs energy, talking, household tasks, mental and manual work. The activities of standing and sleeping take energy. Digested products of food unite with the oxygen which has been released in the breakdown of that food as also with that taken in on the breath, and the result is the release of heat, and the production of new tissue. This heat supplies the energy for work, and is a part of the process of metabolism. The actual work of digestion uses energy. The body cannot utilize all the food it eats and some is excreted as waste: that, too, requires energy.

TABLE OF COMPARATIVE FOOD VALUES

		Protein %	Fat %	Available Carbohydrate %	Water %
*Butter		0·4	85·1	Trace	13·9
Cheese	Cheddar	24·9	34·5	,,	37·0
	Dutch	28·1	16·8	,,	46·3
	Gorgonzola	24·8	31·1	,,	41·0
	St. Ivel	23·1	30·5	,,	45·7
	Stilton	25·1	40·0	,,	28·2
	Gruyère	36·8	33·4	,,	21·9
	Cream cheese	3·2	42·0	2·4	53·0
Eggs	Boiled	11·9	12·3	Nil	73·4
	Poached	12·4	11·7	,,	74·7
Milk	Dried	26·4	29·7	38·8	1·3
	Fresh Milk	3·3	3·7	4·8	87·0
Nuts	Almonds	20·5	53·5	4·3	4·7
(all	Barcelonas	12·9	64·0	5·2	5·7
shelled)	Brazils	13·8	61·5	4·1	8·5
	†Cashews	21·5	52·5	5(approx.)	7·2
	Chestnuts	2·3	2·7	36·6	51·7
	Peanuts	28·1	49·0	8·6	4·5
	Walnuts	12·5	51·5	5·0	23·5
Beans	Broad, boiled	4·1	Trace	7·1	83·7
	Butter, ,,	7·1	,,	17·1	70·5
	French, ,,	0·8	,,	1·1	95·5
	Haricot, ,,	6·6	,,	16·6	69·6
	Runner, ,,	0·8	,,	0·9	93·6
Peas	Fresh, boiled	5·0	Trace	7·7	80·0
	Dried ,,	6·9	,,	19·1	70·3
	Split, dried, boiled	8·3	,,	21·9	67·3
Soya	flour, full fat	40·3	23·5	26·6‡	7·0
	flour, grits	49·6	7·2	34·4‡	7·0
Flour	brown, mixed grist	11·6	1·9	74·2	15·0
	Bread made from it	8·3	1·4	53·3	39·0

* Average figures taken from English, Empire and Foreign samples.

† After removal of brown pericarp.

‡ And dextrin.

		Protein %	Fat %	Available Carbohydrate %	Water %
Flour	mixed grist (80%)	11·2	1·4	77·6	15·0
	Bread made from it	8·3	1·0	57·5	37·0
	mixed grist, white (70%)	10·8	1·1	78·9	15·0
	Bread made from it	8·1	0·8	59·3	36·0
Oatmeal	raw	12·1	8·7	72·8	8·9
Bacon	back rashers, fried	24·6	53·4		12·7
	gammon, fried	31·3	33·9		24·9
Beef	steak, raw	19·3	10·5		68·3
	steak, grilled	25·2	21·6		50·5
	topside, roast, lean and fat	24·2	23·8		50·0
Chicken	boiled, flesh	26·2	10·3		61·0
Mutton	chop, lean, grilled	26·5	17·5		53·7
	leg, roast	25·0	20·4		52·4
Kidney	ox, raw	17·0	5·3		75·5
	sheep, raw	16·8	3·1		77·4
Liver	raw, mixed samples	16·5	8·1		73·3
Cod	middle cut, steamed	18·0	0·9		79·2
Cod	grilled, with added butter	27·0	5·3		64·6
Plaice	raw fillets	15·3	1·8		80·8
	steamed, body of fish	18·1	1·9		78·0

Mineral ash, etc., additional.

Statistics from *Chemical Composition of Foods* by McCance and Widdowson, published by H.M.S.O., and from *Biochemical Journal*, **30**, 1936, for cashew nuts.

V

The body's need of Mineral Elements: Foods which supply these elements

THE mineral elements present in the composition of the human body, in addition to carbon, hydrogen, and oxygen, consist of major amounts of calcium, phosphorus, potassium, sulphur, chlorine, sodium, and magnesium, and of very much smaller amounts of iron, manganese, iodine. Many others are essential constituents, but only in "trace" amounts, and of these the more usually recognized are cobalt, silicon, aluminium, arsenic, boron, copper, fluorine, nickel, and zinc.

Though the amounts present vary considerably from approximately 2 lb. of calcium to only 2·8 grammes of iron and 0·028 grammes of iodine,[1] this is no measurement of their value in the human body, for without its calcium there would be no structure, and without its iron there would be no blood.

It is probable that all the constituents of the atmosphere, the seas, and the soils, enter in infinitesimal amounts into living physical tissue, through the food and the breath, and are essential for full function. These are not all traceable in discernible amounts in human tissue, but it has been found that many diseases have been cured when given an extremely high potency, i.e. a very fine trituration of a "trace" element to act as a synergist, a co-ordinating element, to another factor in the prescription.

This is seen to be true when a minute amount of the trace element arsenic is added to a prescription of Kali. Phos.

[1] 0·09 oz. of iron, and 0·0009 oz. of iodine.

Without the arsenic the Kali. Phos. remains inert in those individuals whose phosphorus metabolism requires this synergist. Sufferers with chronic asthma may require just this metabolism correction.

The mineral elements the body has most need of are calcium and phosphorus, iron and iodine. If the supplies of these are adequate it may be considered that the body's mineral requirements are *probably* being met. Foods which contain calcium, phosphorus, and iron cover a relatively wide range, and those other essential mineral constituents of the physical tissues are generally found in association with them. The iodine requirement may well need separate consideration.

In nature, these mineral elements, the various vitamins, and various "trace" elements are absorbed into the tissues of the plants, animals, fish, and a variety of food in the daily meals is most likely to provide all the factors which the physical tissues need for healthy metabolism. If the meals are deficient in various of these food factors, some part of the metabolic process will suffer, with a sub-standard of nutrition in the cell life, the digestive juices, or the intercellular fluids.

If inflammation and disease invade the physical tissues, disturbing the mineral particles, these mineral elements and the required "trace" elements, when correctly prepared and prescribed as tissue remedies, effect a particular balance, which if not already irrevocable – and this is unusual if taken in time – can be expected to restore health. Suitable nutrition becomes a co-operative factor.

Calcium and Phosphorus

The mineral element most extensively found in the human body is calcium. Every adult needs approximately 0·8 grammes of calcium daily. Additional calcium is needed by women when pregnant, during lactation – since some of their own calcium is given with the milk – and by growing children. These additional needs have been estimated to bring these requirements to a level of 1·4 grammes daily.

The body excretes about 0·5 grammes of calcium daily;

and the 0·3 grammes of the estimated normal daily requirement for adults has to provide the necessary margin to meet all the body's demands.

The body distributes its intake of calcium not only to the bones and teeth, which are formed of calcium and phosphorus in the growing stages, and are constantly having their calcium replaced, but also to the blood for the process of normal clotting, the digestive juice, and to the organic tissues, including the heart muscle: calcium is a factor in ensuring muscular contraction.

Calcium combines with albumen to form new blood cells, bone tissue, and teeth tissue, though this does not necessarily appear in the adult as a new set of teeth. The process after growth is completed is one of renewal. Renewed gastric juice is also formed from the combination of calcium with albumen.

Foods having a high content of calcium are easily remembered, being skimmed milk powders, cheese, eggs, fish in which the bones are edible, and watercress. One pint of milk gives 0·68 grammes; one egg will give approximately 0·45 grammes; and cheese should give 0·23 grammes per oz. Analysed figures for foods with the highest content of calcium are:

	mg. per oz.
Skimmed milk powder	348
Fresh milk	34
Cheese	230
Eggs	17 (per *oz.*)
Whitebait	240
Tinned sardines	113
Watercress	63
National and white breads	30
Herrings	28
Cabbage	18
Turnips	17
Cauliflower	14
Cod	7
Wholemeal bread (100% extraction)	6

Where there is an unbalance in calcium distribution, or a

definite deficiency in the calcium intake, either slight or serious deficiency diseases result.

If too much sugar is taken, the blood is robbed of its calcium. This is because the body attempts to neutralize the effects of excess sugar by drawing on the calcium already present in the blood, the teeth, joints, etc. Excess sugar will also rob the body tissues of oxygen, which it demands for its combustion in the tissues. But the body's oxygen is needed for all its moderate demands, including that of carrying minerals and vitamins to all its tissues.

Too much fat in the diet will prevent full absorption of its calcium. The presence of oxalic acid and phytic acid in certain foods also prevents full calcium absorption. Oxalic acid is notably found in spinach and in rhubarb, and if these two products are served with calcium foods – cheese, eggs, milk custards – the oxalic acid combines with the calcium and forms an insoluble salt, calcium oxalate. It is probable, however, that if a sufficiently liberal amount of cheese or the milk custard is taken with these foods, the additional calcium intake will more than compensate for the insoluble calcium oxalate.

The same neutralization should be observed in serving wholemeal bread with cheese, because of the phytates in the bread and whole-grain cereals, e.g. oatmeal with milk. Some of the phytic acid present with the calcium content in pulse vegetables and whole-grain cereals, however, is destroyed in the various cooking processes these foods may be subjected to.

Effective assimilation of calcium foods may require a prescription of Nat. Mur., especially if there is some gastric trouble, or in convalescence after illness.

The elderly frequently suffer from insufficient calcium and this sometimes occasions the rheumatic-like pains in their muscles and joints. If bones break easily in persons of all ages, and if fractures are slow to heal, this is generally an indication for the need of additional calcium.

The absorption of adequate amounts of calcium by the human body and its distribution in the blood and tissues depends upon its intake of phosphorus, the presence of vitamin D, and the normal activity of the parathyroid glands. These glands act as a balancing mechanism in controlling the calcium level in the blood. This level should remain constant, the bones acting as a "bank" from which calcium for the blood can be withdrawn, or where excess calcium can be temporarily deposited.

Phosphorus is found in close association with calcium and the question of adequate supplies does not arise irrespective of the calcium intake. Not only is phosphorus concerned closely with calcium in the formation of bones and teeth and in their renewal processes, but it assists in the processes of the body's metabolism by which energy is released from its food. Phosphorus also stabilizes the composition of the body's fluids.

There is a good content of phosphorus in almost all foods: those which give the highest figures are:

	mg. per oz.	
Cheese	155	
Oatmeal	108	
Eggs	62	(per oz.)
National bread	28	
Milk	28	
Cabbage	18	

Vitamin D assists in correcting the ratio of calcium to phosphorus supply taken from food. The presence of vitamin D in the body is essential for the successful absorption of calcium. A small intake of calcium in the daily meals, having the vitamin D factor also present is of greater value to the body than a large amount of calcium without its co-operating factor, vitamin D. The vitamin D present renders the small amount of calcium wholly assimilable: a large amount of calcium if taken with insufficient vitamin D being present will probably register in a calcium deficiency. Where there is insufficient vitamin D, there is sure to be signs of calcium deficiency

Vitamin D also promotes the health of the skin: sunlight, and ultra-violet irradiation are used therapeutically for certain skin diseases. Vitamin D is manufactured within the body by the action of sunlight on the skin, by the use of ultra-violet lamps – exposure needs careful supervision – and by the inclusion of foods which contain this vitamin in the daily meals. This vitamin is not found in many foods: it is, however, resistant to cooking processes and no loss need be expected. Foods which contain this vitamin are:

International Units per oz.

Tunny fish oil	Used as dietary supplements and for therapeutic purposes 5,400, 5,670, and above, per oz.
Halibut liver oil	
Cod liver oil	
Sardines	280
Herrings	250
Tinned salmon	170
Margarine (added synthetically)	90
Eggs	17 (per *oz.*)
Butter	17
Cheese	4
Milk (fresh)	0·1–0·7 (seasonal variation)

Some milk powders have added vitamin content and details are given on their labels.

The adult requirement for vitamin D has not been fixed, and it would be extremely difficult to make a general assessment. If, however, an adult is suffering from nutritional debility, or has a deficiency disease because of some unbalance in assimilation (poor assimilation of calcium is probably a contributing factor in some cases of rheumatism), additional vitamin D is generally indicated.

The daily requirement for this vitamin by growing children has been estimated as 500 International Units. It is considered correct that the elderly are able to convert calcium from any such deposits within their tissues up to a late age. Obviously to do this adequate amounts of vitamin D are required, and it would appear unwise to estimate the required intake as very much lower than 500 I.U. for any age. The vitamin is concerned also in preventing caries of the teeth, a point which can become of increasing interest to all ages.

The body is able to store this vitamin to draw upon as its needs require.

Calcium occurs in the body in two forms, calcium carbonate, and calcium phosphate. This latter is the compound of calcium and phosphorus. The body's requirement for calcium and phosphorus is closely related.

Calcium carbonate is considered a suitable form of calcium for adding to wheat flours, other than the 100 per cent extraction. The argument is that the added calcium offsets the harmful effects of the phytates present in the higher extraction flours, and needs to be added to the low-extraction (white) flours on account of their de-mineralization in the milling process.

The 100 per cent extraction wheat flour free of the added calcium carbonate was agreed to in response to a minority's plea that their bread should be neither added to nor subjected to de-mineralization processes.

It seems a pity, however, that calcium phosphate and silica in a potency of possibly 3x cannot be introduced in preference to the calcium carbonate. This procedure would be likely to retard ageing, since in the tissues of old people their silica content diminishes and carbonates form in their place – this being, in fact, a process of ageing.

Iron

The iron requirement of the body has been given as 0·004 per cent of the body's weight. The average amount found in the body of a man weighing 11 st. is 0·09 oz. or 2·8 grammes. Authoritative figures give the needs of adult men and women for iron as 12 milligrams a day, with adolescents, nursing mothers, and those in pregnancy needing 15 milligrams.

The body is able to store very little of its iron, and foods containing this requirement should be included in the daily meals. In general, these foods are whole-grain flours, whole-grain cereals, egg-yolk, beef liver, green vegetables and some fruits.

Some of the iron in food is not assimilable, but inorganic iron is absorbed and in this form it occurs in certain fruits, in green vegetables, in liver, kidney, in white fish, and in eggs. Insufficient hydrochloric acid in the digestive juices may prevent iron absorption from even the assimilable iron foods.

Iron is apparently best absorbed by the physical tissues in the form of ferrous iron, and it is the presence of ascorbic acid – vitamin C – in the intestine which facilitates its absorption by changing one form of iron into another, the ferric ions into ferrous ions.

The limited storage of iron in the body, and its utilization as required by the tissues depend upon the substance apoferritin in the intestinal mucous membrane. The full capacity of this protein for taking up iron is easily reached, and in consequence the body's supplies of assimilable iron need daily replenishment through well-chosen foods. It will be appreciated also that intestinal health is a contributing feature of iron absorption.

The following table gives a list of foods with a good iron content, and, as well, the percentage rate of this which is assimilable iron. Those foods with the highest content are marked with an asterisk for easier reference. The other foods shown in this list, when used during the full complement of the day's meals, provide a useful contribution to that day's assimilable iron content. For purposes of interest and comparison, some figures for flesh foods are also included. These contain good sources of organic iron, but, as will be seen, little of this is actually assimilable by the body.

These figures may show small variations for the several foodstuffs, but the authors of the analysis advise us that they can be accepted with confidence (*Biochemic Journal*, **30**). Figures for raw and cooked food are given in some cases to show small variations in the figure content when subjected to cooking and other processes.

Note. – Sherman's figures give the daily standard allowance as 1·32 grammes phosphorus, 0·68 grammes calcium, 0·012 grammes iron: *Chemistry of Food and Nutrition*, by H. C. Sherman.

TABLE OF FOODS SHOWING THE TOTAL IRON IN MG.
PER 100 G. OF THE FOOD: ALSO THE PERCENTAGE OF
THE TOTAL IRON WHICH IS ASSIMILABLE

	Total iron in mg. per 100 g.	Assimilable iron % of total iron
Vegetables:		
Artichoke, globe, cooked	0·55	100
Beans, broad, raw	*1·08	93
butter, cooked	*1·82	71
French, raw	0·57	87
haricot, cooked	*2·72	84
scarlet runner, cooked	*0·74	74
tinned, baked	*2·05	98
Beetroot, cooked	0·50	94
Brussels sprouts, raw	0·67	75
Cabbage, cooked	0·87	70
Carragheen moss	*8·88	97
Carrot, raw	*0·56	100
cooked	0·41	98
Cauliflower, cooked	0·52	100
Celeriac, cooked	*0·87	98
Celery, raw	0·14	100
Chicory, raw	0·57	66
Cucumber, raw	0·25	100
Endive, raw	*2·77	72
Fennel, raw, fresh	*4·20	50
raw, dry	*9·06	45
Leek, raw	*0·77	91
Lentil, raw	*7·63	60
Lettuce, raw	0·80	63
Mushroom, raw	0·65	100
Mustard and cress, raw	*5·70	45
Parsley, raw	*10·00	50
Peas, cooked	*1·55	77
split, cooked	*1·84	71
tinned	*2·10	100
Radish, raw	*1·68	65
Salsify, raw	*1·33	98
Sea kale	0·66	91
Spinach, cooked	*4·15	67

C

	Total iron in mg. per 100 g.	Assimilable iron % of total iron
Watercress, raw	*2·08	66
Fruits:		
Apricot, dry, raw	*4·08	98
fresh, raw	0·37	95
Avocado pear, raw	0·53	100
Banana, raw	0·47	100
Blackberry, raw	0·95	41
Cherry, raw	0·48	100
Currant, black, raw	*0.95	100
red, raw	0·66	85
Custard apple, raw	0·52	100
Damson, raw	0·63	70
Date, dry	*1·71	82
Fig, dry, raw	*4·17	96
Grape, as raisins	*3·80	97
as sultana	*3·60	65
Greengage, raw	0·46	84
Loganberry, raw	*1·00	76
Medlar, raw	0·77	65
Mulberry, raw	1·57	50
Nectarine, raw	0·46	87
Passion fruit, raw	*1·12	100
Peach, dry, raw	*7.60	92
fresh, raw	0·39	100
Plum, as prunes, raw	*3·20	72
Raspberry, raw	*1·11	82
Strawberry	0·71	52
Tomato, raw	0·37	53
Nuts:		
Almond	*4·54	99
Barcelona	*3·44	91
Brazil	*2·70	61
Cob	*1·44	94
Chestnut	0·87	60
Peanut	*1·19	100
Walnut	*1·83	41
Coconut	*1·98	86

	Total iron in mg. per 100 g.	Assimilable iron % of total iron
Cereals:		
Biscuit, digestive	*1·57	91
Ryvita	*3·20	100
Bread, wholemeal	*3·43	83
"Hovis"	*2·48	95
Oatmeal	*4·15	96
Miscellaneous:		
Cocoa	*14.20	93
Chocolate, plain	*1·67	84
milk	*3·28	89
Treacle, Golden Syrup	*1·68	95
Black	*9·17	100
Egg, raw	*2·50	100
Flesh foods:		
Fish, Cod, raw	0·34	100
Haddock, steamed	*0.75	100
Halibut, raw	0·44	100
Herring, fried	*1·02	74
Mackerel, fried	*1·17	64
Plaice, steamed	0·68	97
Salmon, tinned	*0·89	94
Sardines, tinned	*3·44	65
Skate, raw	0·33	100
Sole, steamed	0·45	100
Winkles, boiled	*10·4	58
Heart, baked	*5·83	63
Kidney, ox, stewed	*4·92	66
pig, fried	*9·50	58
Liver, calf's, raw	*13·30	100
lamb's, fried	*2·76	100
ox, raw	*6·70	78
pig's, raw	*20·00	80
Sweetbreads, raw	*1·47	71

Flesh foods having good organic iron content, but low percentages of assimilable iron:	*Total iron in mg. per* 100 *g.*	*Assimilable iron* % *of total iron*
Beef, roast	5·20	22
corned, tinned	3·34	35
Chicken, white flesh, roast	1·60	31
red flesh, roast	2·70	24
Mutton, roast	5·10	24
Veal, roast	1·35	55
Bacon, raw	2·50	29
Pork chop, fried	1·40	47
Tongue, cooked	5·80	19
Rabbit, stewed	1·89	42

Iodine

Only a very minute amount of iodine is needed by human tissues, the daily requirement being given by Professor V. H. Mottram as 75 microgrammes, which is 75 one-millionth parts of a gramme.[1] Iodine is, however, essential for the correct functioning of the thyroid gland. This gland controls the rate of metabolism and that of normal growth of children. Lack of iodine causes the thyroid gland to enlarge, a condition recognizable as goitre. An enlargement of the gland happens during pregnancy and lactation, when additional iodine is needed, and foods containing iodine should be specially included in the day's meals. Children need additional iodine during the period of adolescence.

Drinking water should contain traces of iodine – except in those areas where the soil is iodine-free – as will milk taken from cows which feed on pasturage where the soil contains iodine. The richest sources are sea-foods – fish, and the edible seaweeds. Where iodine occurs in the soil, the watercress and onions grown there will be the richest vegetable sources.

Sodium and Chlorine are recognizably taken as salt at table, and constitute that element in salted foods. This combination element – sodium chloride – is essential in the production of

[1] *Food Sense*, edited by Professor V. H. Mottram.

healthy gastric juice and a good digestion. Its function in the blood is to assist in carrying carbon dioxide to the lungs. Most people eat far more salt than they need, and since the body has difficulty in absorbing the coarse division of most salts taken with food, a sodium chloride deficiency is not uncommon. Biochemic preparations of salt for the table are to be preferred to the use of a coarse table salt, and molecular doses of Nat. Mur. can be expected to adjust an unbalance in the body tissues and fluids. (See Nat. Mur., page 37.)

Those who are engaged in heavy work which induces considerable sweating, who take strenuous exercise, or who live in hot climates, require a higher salt intake. If any of these conditions induces muscular cramp, it is a symptom that too much salt has been lost from the body, and a saline drink is indicated.

It has been estimated that adults need 4 grammes of salt daily, and the average intake has been given as 15 grammes: the body normally excretes excess salt in the urine and through the sweat.

Potassium has an affinity for the muscle cells and in the blood becomes a constituent of the red blood cells. It is not lost in sweat and is excreted only in the urine, approximately three grammes daily being lost in this way. Most foods contain potassium, except tripe, tapioca, sago, fats, and the processed starches – such as arrowroot, polished rice. These foods have little or no potassium content. Good sources of potassium in foods are given below:

	mg. per oz.[1]
Cod, steamed	102
Mutton chop, raw	100
Beefsteak, raw	95
Herring, raw	90
Milk	71
Eggs	39 (per *oz.*)
Cheddar cheese	33
Cornflakes	32

Figures given in *Manual of Nutrition*, published H.M.S.O.

Human tissues need *sulphur*. The inorganic element is an essential factor in carrying oxygen more particularly to the skin. Sulphur occurs as a protein compound, and eggs and fish are the best sources: vitamin B_1, and whole-grain proteins also contain this element.

Magnesium is found in almost all foods. This mineral is a constituent of the bones and teeth, it nourishes all nerve tissue, and in association with calcium and phosphorus it gives elasticity to muscle tissue. Magnesium promotes ease and relaxation of nervous tension, and those who are troubled with symptoms of acidity may need remedial doses of this mineral.

Manganese is related to the iron content in human tissues, and a dilution as a nutrient will increase the iron in the blood and tissues. Manganese is found in nuts, whole-grain cereals, and in teas.

So very minute an amount is required by the human body of *fluorine* that this becomes a "trace" element. It is essential in the composition of sound bones and teeth, and apparently the advisable intake is 0·3–0·5 parts of fluorine per million. This marginal figure should give good results only and produce excellent teeth. Larger amounts are likely to cause a mottling of the teeth, and poisoning results – as is the case with "trace" elements – when this element occurs in excess.

Fluorine is a constituent of most drinking water, and the content is generally in strict control.

Copper is an essential "trace" element in human tissues, necessary in the formation of haemoglobin, and acting as a catalyst, that is, it produces a required chemical reaction without which the necessary process would not be activated. Its function in this connexion is to keep up the number of red corpuscles in the blood, preventing an anaemia.

Copper also assists the iron in the blood as a carrier of oxygen to the tissues. Many foods contain a trace of copper, and the best sources are liver, nuts, peas, beans, most fruits, and green vegetables.

Zinc is found in most foods. It is an essential element in the body's production of insulin, and is needed in regulating the body's sugar metabolism. It also assists the blood in carrying carbon dioxide to the lungs for elimination.

Water is an essential nutritional factor. It is the major constituent of the blood and the digestive juices, and the day's food can only be absorbed in solution. The body eliminates approximately $4\frac{1}{2}$ pints each day, and this replacement is obtained in the proportions of about one-third from solid food, $\frac{3}{4}$ pint from the absorption and assimilation of this food, and the remainder – 2–3 pints of fluid – is taken in the form of various drinks. In conditions of fever and diarrhoeas a higher intake of fluid is needed and a natural water is the best choice to give. Those who take strenuous exercise or who live in hot climates will of course require a higher intake of fluid to compensate for the increased loss from greater perspiration.

VI

Vitamins in Food

VITAMINS are accessory food factors producing necessary chemical reactions when in association with related elements. Thus, the presence of vitamin D in association with calcium and phosphorus is the essential factor in effecting the chemical reactions for calcium-phosphorus absorption in the human tissues. Similarly, vitamin B_{12}, having the trace element cobalt within itself, is vitally important in pernicious anaemia. (Cobalt is frequently the vital link in the iron-cobalt-copper chain of elements required in blood making.)

Vitamins are present in natural foods before these have been purified for experimental purposes or for popular taste, or have been subjected to second-rate cooking processes, or – as is particularly the case with vitamin C – largely lost in the staling and bruising of the living plant.

When food is persistently taken which does not contain the full complement of these vitamins, and the essential minerals, mild or serious conditions of deficiency soon become apparent and subnormal health and disease result. In these cases, feeding with those foods which do contain sufficient of these necessary factors is of major assistance in restoring optimum health.

Each of the vitamins necessary to human nutrition has its own particular function, but several are in close relationship in their nutritional processes. This is so of vitamins A, C, and D, which are all associated with the calcium and phosphorus intake in promoting the growth of bone structure and the renewal processes in gastric juice, soft tissues, and mucous membranes.

Where the community is reasonably well fed, any vitamin deficiency is most apparent in early spring after the lack of sunshine and young green vegetable produce sustained during the winter months. Most of the summer's vitamin D store within the tissues has been utilized unless this has meanwhile been supplemented by specially chosen foods or vitamin capsules. Vitamin C is predominant in the sprouting points of green vegetables, for example sprouting broccoli, and in all young growing produce. Some supplies of lettuce, cress, and other saladings are grown under glass, but the main crops come with the spring. Garden and wayside herbs, too, cannot be said to have their full content of vitamin C before they start into their spring growth. Part of the necessary vitamin C content in food can be obtained from fresh fruit and from summer supplies that have been suitably bottled for winter use.

Unhealthy conditions of the bowel, and particularly diarrhoea, will cause loss of vitamins and mineral nutrients. The use of medicinal paraffin, especially if taken soon after food, will carry through the bowel both its contents and the vitamins there which have not been given time for intestinal absorption, even supposing the natural secretions and micro-organisms of the colon are sufficiently active to promote this essential nutrition.

The important vitamins for human well-being are the fat-soluble A, D, E, and K, and those which are water-soluble, the vitamin B complex, and vitamins C and P.

In vitamin A we have essentially a protective factor, since where the intake of this vitamin is inadequate, human tissues easily take infectious diseases. This vitamin has a special relationship with all the epithelial tissues, the lining cells which protect all organs and body tissues, and a deficiency of the vitamin results in poor stamina of these protective cells. This is seen in easy infection to colds, influenza, measles, bronchitis, gastric influenza, mumps, diseases in which the protective tissues of the skin, the eyes, the lungs, sinuses, the digestive organs, and the glands are variously involved.

A serious deficiency of vitamin A results in deterioration and consequent ulceration of the membrane of the eyes, with blindness if the condition is not corrected in time.

Exhaustive research work has established the amount of this vitamin needed daily by the various sections of the community. The adult person and children in their 'teens require 5,000 International Units, but a youth of eighteen years or so will require 6,000 I.U. This figure has also been arrived at for the expectant mother, but during lactation her requirements are increased to 8,000 I.U. Young children of two years or more will need 2,000 I.U., but at five years old they will need rather more at 2,500 I.U. per day.

There are two forms of this vitamin in food. That which occurs in vegetable produce is known as the vegetable vitamin A, and from animal, fish, or dairy products as the animal vitamin A. Much of the intake of the vegetable vitamin A is used in the actual assimilation of this food factor, more from some vegetable sources than others, and it is generally estimated that only one-third of the intake from this source is available to the tissues. The recommendation is the proportion of one-third of the animal vitamin and two-thirds of the vegetable vitamin.

This vitamin is not destroyed by cooking or the processes of canning.

The body does not use more vitamin A than it needs, but any additional intake is stored in the liver and then used later against a seasonal deficiency

Vitamin A in food

It is difficult to give exact figures for the vitamin A content in various foods since appreciable variation is shown from the samples tested, and in the figures given by two such undoubted authorities as Professor V. H. Mottram in *Food Sense*, and H.M.S.O. publication, *Manual of Nutrition*. There is quite a wide seasonal variation, the vitamin content of the milk and butter falling low during the English winter compared with the high vitamin content when the animals are fed on a rich pasturage. Soil conditions and the amount of sunshine probably accounts for variations in the figures from the vegetable sources. The following figures appear to be valid:

Animal A	*I.U. per oz.*
Ox liver	4,255
New Zealand butter	1,140
English butter, summer	1,000
winter	255
Cheese, Cheddar	369
Eggs	280
Kidney	280
Condensed milk (whole milk)	105
Sardines	70
Herrings	42
Fresh milk, summer	195
winter	8
Halibut liver oil	600,000 (average)
Cod liver oil	30,000 (,,)

Vegetable A	
Parsley	3,690
Spinach	3,000
Turnip tops	2,130
Carrots	1,730–5,197
Kale	1,570
Dried apricots	1,420
Tomatoes	800
Dried prunes	600
Watercress	475–1,418
Cabbage	180

Small amounts of the vitamin are contained in fresh apricots, peaches, plums and greengages, and in green peas. The dark green leaves of vegetables contain more of this vitamin, carotene, than the inner and paler leaves.

Vitamin A is synthetically added to margarine: the figures given by Professor Mottram are 450–550 I.U. per oz., and in the H.M.S.O. publication, 850 I.U. per oz., which indicates a wide variation in the samples tested.

Vitamin D

The function of vitamin D is so closely related to calcium and phosphorus metabolism that it has been dealt with in discussing those elements. (See pages 58–63.) Foods which contain this vitamin again show a seasonal variation, and almost the only natural sources are shown below:

	I.U. per oz.[1]
Halibut liver oil	5,400–114,000
Cod liver oil	5,670
Sardines	280
Herring	250
Tinned salmon	170 (average)
Eggs	17 („)
Butter	3–28
Cheese	4–10
Milk	0·3 (average)
Margarine has the vitamin added synthetically to	90

The B complex of vitamins

The B complex of vitamins consists of food factors affecting particularly the nervous system, and the metabolism of carbohydrates. If the end-product of this metabolism, glucose, is not properly oxidized – through the agency of the B_1 vitamin – these products circulate in the blood and poison the nervous system. The amounts needed of this vitamin are in relation to the amount of carbohydrate eaten. Whole-grain foods are good sources of the vitamin and more than balance their carbohydrate content. Meats contain this

[1] Both Professor Mottram's figures and the H.M.S.O. *Manual of Nutrition* have been consulted.

vitamin, and fruits and vegetables balance their carbohydrate contents. Yeast preparations and wheat germ foods are excellent sources of the vitamin.

The taking of sulphonamide drugs renders this vitamin, and the microbes which synthesize it in the body, inactive.

The B_2 vitamin, now generally known as Riboflavin, is specially vital to the body's digestive processes. An insufficiency in the daily meals over a period of time causes nervous depression, easy infection to disease, the skin becomes unhealthy, and vision suffers. Generous amounts of this vitamin bring robustness to children. It is a catalyst, a reactive agent, in the assimilation of food products, and increases growth in children.

Nicotinic Acid is the third of these B vitamins: it is called Niacin in America. A slight deficiency of this vitamin is not at all uncommon. The symptoms include a red, sore tongue, with diarrhoea and abdominal pain, accompanied by lassitude and depression. Natural sources of this vitamin are yeast, whole-grain foods, meat and offal, mushrooms, peanuts, eggs, herrings, white fish, and beer.

The other vitamins of this group are Pyridoxine, Pantothenic Acid, Biotin, Folic Acid, Choline, Paramino-benzoic Acid, Inositol, and vitamin B_{12}. With the exception of the Folic Acid factor and vitamin B_{12} they are of secondary importance in general nutrition as they are usually found in flours which contain the germ and the husk, in natural unpolished rice, and in milk, eggs, and vegetables, and a number of these foods normally are included in the daily meals.

The Folic Acid factor is vitally important in certain forms of anaemia, and is found in the leaves of green vegetables and saladings, in yeast, in liver and in kidney, and meals specially inclusive of these foods need to be given to sufferers with this disease.

The vitamin B_{12} is unusual in that it contains the trace element cobalt. Research on the nature of this vitamin continues: it is claimed that B_{12} restores the blood picture to normal in pernicious anaemia and has a good effect on the accompanying disability of the nervous system. This is most probably effected by the presence of the trace element cobalt within the vitamin.

B_{12} is apparently the only vitamin in the B group the body is able to store. The liver is able to do this since B_{12} is in combination with a protein and an enzyme: this compound prevents pernicious anaemia.

All conditions of diarrhoea, and the taking of purgatives interferes with the activity of the B group of vitamins; similarly, while sulphonamide drugs are being taken. Sunlight destroys the Riboflavin content in milk when it is left so exposed.

Only a little of the B_1 and Riboflavin vitamins are lost in dry cooking processes, but the alkalis in baking powder and raising agents will destroy some of the vitamin content in making cakes and scones. The B_1, Riboflavin, and Nicotinic Acid easily dissolve in cooking liquids, but if a small amount of this liquid is used to make soup or gravy enriched with these vitamins, the whole is then used at the meal.

DAILY REQUIREMENTS OF VITAMIN B

The daily requirements for this vitamin group by the various sections of the community are different for the separate vitamins.

The intake for B_1 needed by sedentary workers is at least 1·1 milligrams each day; an active adult needs at least 1·5 milligrams; an expectant mother 1·8 milligrams; and the very active man and the nursing mother require at least 2·0 milligrams daily. A child of 2 years needs 0·6 milligrams, at 5 years old the requirement is 0·8 milligrams, and at 14 years 1·3 milligrams are needed; a youth of 18 who engages in strenuous sport will need at least 1·8 milligrams.

The requirement for Riboflavin (vitamin B_2) is about half as much again as for vitamin B_1 for each of the various sections of the community. Some part of this is manufactured within the tissues of healthy subjects, but it is estimated that the daily requirement is from 1·6 to 2·6 milligrams according to age and occupation.

The requirement for Nicotinic Acid is at least 12–20 milligrams a day: it is advisable to increase this during pregnancy and lactation. The activity of microbes in the large intestine both manufacture and destroy the vitamin. If much energy is expended and a larger amount of food consumed, the higher figure for intake is needed to provide the link in the metabolism of carbohydrates taken.

As will be seen from the table of natural sources, yeast and yeast products provide the highest content of these vitamins.

Natural sources of vitamin B_1.[1]

	mg. per oz.
Dried brewers' yeast	2·75
Bacon	0·17
Oatmeal	0·13
Green peas	0·12
Peanuts, roasted	0·07
Wholemeal bread (100% extraction)	0·07
Mutton	0·05
White bread	0·04
Potato	0·03
Beef	0·02
Cabbage	0·02
Milk	0·01

Natural sources of Riboflavin[1]

Dried brewer's yeast	1·54
Liver	0·85
Cheese	0·14
Egg	0·11
Beef	0·07
Milk	0·04
Wholemeal bread (100% extraction)	0·03
Potato	0·02

[1] These figures are given in H.M.S.O. *Manual of Nutrition.*

Natural sources of Nicotinic Acid[1]

	mg. per oz.
Dried brewer's yeast	10·3
Liver, kidney	3·8
Beef	1·3
Bacon	1·1
Wholemeal bread (100% extraction)	1·2
Peanuts, roasted	0·6
Cod	0·6
Beer	0·4
Potato	0·3
White bread	0·3
Cabbage	0·1

The High Value of Vitamin C

This vitamin is also known as Ascorbic Acid: its presence in the body protects the tissues from scurvy. Symptoms of a slight deficiency in the intake of this vitamin occur frequently, for many people do not take sufficient of the foods which contain it. Symptoms of this deficiency are irritability, sore gums, tissues easily bruise, rheumatism-like pains in the joints, lack of stamina, slow or interrupted growth in children, and lack of resistance to infection – whatever it may be.

This vitamin is associated with vitamins A and D and the minerals calcium and phosphorus in the balance of metabolism in human tissues, and in the promotion of good bone structure and healthy teeth. Vitamin C assists also in the assimilation of food carbohydrates and in the correct activity of heart and muscle tissue.

The presence of vitamin C promotes healing after surgical treatment, including the extraction of teeth. It is, as well, a protective vitamin in neutralizing the poison from the tuberculosis germ. And, in addition, it assists the absorption of iron. (See page 64.)

Research indicates that adults need at least 20 milligrams daily of this vitamin: American standards aim at 75 milligrams daily. Sufferers with rheumatoid arthritis, and those

---

[1] These figures are given in H.M.S.O. *Manual of Nutrition.*

with any fever are likely to need 40 to 50 milligrams daily. Elderly people seldom have sufficient of this vitamin.

Health suffers from even temporary shortages of this vitamin. This is particularly likely to happen in the late winter months and early spring before the young saladings and sprouting vegetables are in good supply. There is a higher vitamin C content in the growing points of green vegetables, and in the young growing leaves of chives and dandelions than when mature; the skins of oranges, tomatoes, and apples have a higher content of the vitamin – provided these fruits have been recently gathered – than the pulp. Loss of the vitamin occurs as the skin shrivels. The highest content of the vitamin is in growing produce just before coming to maturity or ripening. Stored foods gradually decrease in their vitamin content, whether these be green vegetables, roots, or fruit.

SPECIAL CARE AGAINST LOSS OF VITAMIN C

Vitamin C is the most susceptible of all the vitamins to loss. This occurs from the action of its own plant substances and shows in withering, fading, bruising. Loss also occurs in prolonged heating, as in baking, boiling, etc. The vitamin is easily soluble and there is considerable loss when vegetables are left steeped in cold water for more than a short period.

Loss of this vitamin occurs if it comes into contact with copper pans, and if soda is added in cooking green vegetables. Exposure of vegetables to sunlight, once they have been cut and gathered, and keeping milk standing in sunlight, results in loss of the vitamin.

In preparing vegetables for a meal some cell damage is unavoidable. Bruising, cutting, peeling, grating, all cause some cell damage. This releases a plant enzyme which, when in contact with the oxygen of the atmosphere and its vitamin C, destroys its vitamin. The less cutting, and the sharper the knife, the less will be the cell damage, and vitamin loss. All vegetables should be used as soon as possible after the necessary cell damage has occurred, for if they are left standing further loss of the vitamin continues through the enzyme action.

If vegetables are cooked in their skins, this saves vitamin loss.

If the water in which green vegetables are to be cooked has reached boiling point, this temperature ensures that the enzyme itself is destroyed before it destroys the vitamin.

Less cooking time is required if vegetables are coarsely cut and if the roots are cut into large pieces, and by using the minimum of water for the process, there is less continued cooking loss. In addition the content of the minerals and the vitamin leached out into the cooking water will be contained and can be used as a vegetable broth and served as a small drink before the meal. This drink can be enriched with a yeast preparation.

VITAMIN C LOSS IN FRUIT

Fruit is protected by its skin and its own acids and suffers much less loss of its vitamin C than vegetables, though bruising and damage should be avoided. Fruit should be kept cool to sustain its peak perfection just previous to being fully ripe. If fruit has to be cut for later use at table, a light sprinkling with lemon juice prevents further vitamin loss and deterioration.

There is little loss of vitamin C in cooking fruit, and if little water is added the cooking juice is also consumed. The addition of bicarbonate of soda to fruit for any purpose destroys its vitamin C.

SOURCES OF VITAMIN C IN FOODS

	milligrams per oz. of the raw food [1]
Blackcurrants	57·0
Oranges	16·0
Strawberries	16·0
Grapefruit	14·0
Lemon	12·0
Melon	8·5
Raspberries	9·0

[1] This analysis given in *Food Sense*, edited by Professor V. H. Mottram.

milligrams per oz.
of the raw food[1]

Loganberries	9·0
Pineapple	5·7
Cherries, grapes, pears and plums	1·0
Peppers	35·0
Chives	33·0
Brussels sprouts	28·0
Cauliflower	20·0
Cabbage	20·0
Sprouting broccoli	18·5 and higher
Watercress	17·0
Kohlrabi	14·0
Swedes, turnips	7·0
Tomatoes	7·0
Lettuce	4·0
Spring onions, and French beans	3·0
Celery	1·0

THE FUNCTION OF VITAMIN P

This vitamin is found in close association with vitamin C, and has been called vitamin P because it gives permeability to the fine blood vessels. Where there is a lack of this vitamin the blood seeps through the walls of these small vessels and shows in the surrounding tissues as if these had been bruised.

Many vitamin C foods also contain this vitamin – blackcurrants, tomatoes, summer cabbage and lettuce, and rosehip syrup; other fruits which have little or no vitamin C have a good content of vitamin P – apples, plums, and cherries. A good variety of these foods should provide adequate supplies of both these vitamins.

No figure for the daily requirement of vitamin P for human beings has yet been fixed.

Vitamin E

The human requirement for vitamin E is not yet known, and research in connexion with this vitamin continues. It is

[1] This analysis given in *Food Sense*, edited by Professor V. H. Mottram.

thought that it has some influence on cholesterol metabolism and possibly an anti-thrombotic effect.

This vitamin appears to be closely associated with the reproductive system and has been found useful with other measures in preventing habitual abortion, during the menopause, to prolong maturity and avoid ageing of the tissues.

Good natural sources of the vitamin are wheat germ, lettuce, egg-yolk, milk.

Vitamin K

Vitamin K is essential to enable the blood to clot, and is an anti-haemorrhagic vitamin. The vitamin is found in green vegetables, and in green peas, and if the meals contain sufficient supplies of vitamins A and C, this vitamin should automatically be included. There is another substance normally manufactured in the large intestine having this same K activity, called K_2, and if for some reason vitamin K should be absent *temporarily* from the food intake, the body should have this second protective factor within its tissues.

The taking of medicinal paraffin or other similar laxative is likely to impede the manufacture of K_2 within the body.

VII

Therapeutic Section

NOTE: *Certain diseases are notifiable to the Authorities as constituting a source of infection or danger to life. Biochemic treatment can be followed in all conditions of pain and disease at the discretion of the individual concerned but the laws of each country in these matters must of course be complied with.*

INDEX OF TREATMENTS

APPENDICITIS: Give Ferr. Phos., and Kali. Mur., alternately, in half-hourly doses of each, in the 6x or 3–200x potency, with four doses of Mag. Phos., in the 3x or 3–200x potency, during the first day of the illness: give also two doses of Silicea[1] in the 3–200x potency, during this day. Apply hot fomentations, using four doses of the Ferr. Phos., in a small solution.

During subsequent days of the illness, give Ferr. Phos., and Kali. Mur., in a 12x potency or the 3–200x potency in two-hourly doses, and repeat the two doses (morning and afternoon) of the Silicea in the 3–200x potency.

Continue the hot fomentations if these are needed.

No food must be given: give only tepid water to sip. The bowels can be cleansed with an enema using a pint of warm water, provided this can be taken comfortably by the sufferer.

If a putrefactive bowel appears to be the cause of the appendicitis, or is a contributing factor, Kali. Phos. must be given also, at hourly intervals in the 12x or 3–200x potency.

If *Peritonitis* is threatened, having a tympanitic abdomen (drum-like), give half-hourly doses of Kali. Sulph., in a 12x or 3–200x potency, in addition to the doses of Ferr. Phos., and Kali. Mur., as detailed for Appendicitis: but give Kali. Phos. instead of Ferr. Phos. if fever persists.

ARTHRITIS AND RHEUMATISM

ARTHRITIS, having some degree of deformity – Use Silicea and Calc. Fluor. in the 30x potency or the 3–200x, and take one dose of each, morning and evening.

The "crippled" tissues are able to absorb the high potency of these tissue salts and the fibre cells regain some elasticity and strength: in some cases full regeneration is possible, but this depends on several factors, such as age and weight and if the tissues involved have been subjected to continued use and strain.

[1] The use of Silicea needs experience in this condition and may even be contra-indicated.

Where this disease has been present for some years, and these remedies will need to be used for some time, it is advisable to omit the doses entirely, say, on Sundays and on Wednesdays.

In chronic and long-standing conditions of this disease, compound prescriptions incorporating essential trace elements as synergists may be needed.

The daily meals need to be well balanced and little salt should be taken as this is likely to upset the valuable sodium-potassium balance in the tissues. (See also Appendix for comments and menus under Rheumatism and Arthritis, p. 119.)

RHEUMATISM: *Inflammatory conditions* – with soreness or pain in the muscles, or within a joint, generally with swelling and stiffness. The pain is worse on movement of the muscle or joint, and the longer the movement is continued the worse the pain becomes.

Use Ferr. Phos., and Kali. Mur., in alternation, in the 12x potency or the 3–200x; if the condition is acute take five doses of each salt during the day, and as the condition improves take the doses less frequently.

Oxygen-deficient rheumatism with weakness – Joints feel weak, standing is disliked: the pain is worse when warm in bed, or in warm rooms, and in the evenings: pains move around and are in muscles and joints. (Some irregular function of the glands is usually present and foods containing iodine are needed: see chapter on iodine, p. 68.)

Use Kali. Sulph.; use also Mag. Phos. in alternation if the sufferer is a highly-strung person, usually tensed up, or if the pains are usually worse on the right side of the body. Use the 12x potency, or the 3–200x, morning and evening, of one or both remedies, and more often if the condition seems specially acute.

Toxic and "acid" rheumatism – brings pain on movement, but the condition is easier with continued movement. The pain and difficulty of movement is usually worse in the early part of the day, or after a period of rest.

Use Nat. Phos., and Kali. Phos., in alternation, both in the 12x potency or the 3–200x, three times a day between meals.

The Nat. Phos. is the tissue remedy to emulsify the degenerate lactic acid in the tissues causing the pain, and the Kali. Phos. is the remedy for the secondary toxic conditions present in this type of rheumatism.

This condition is usually worse in damp weather or if living in damp conditions, when a dose of Nat. Sulph. in the same potency should be taken in addition each day this is relevant.

Systematic and chronic rheumatism – Take one dose of Silicea daily, in the 12x or the 3–200x potency.

In damp weather take also one dose of Nat. Sulph., in the 12x or the 3–200x potency.

If the condition becomes acute with heat and swelling in any part of the body, see *Inflammatory rheumatism*: see also comments and dosage for *Toxic* and *Oxygen-deficient rheumatisms*.

Refer also to comments on food and the daily menus.

See Appendix for details of relative trace elements; How to Understand Rheumatism and Arthritis; Three Food Dangers; Foods and Menus for use in Rheumatism and Arthritis.

BLOOD DISORDERS: *Abscess, Boils*: Give Ferr. Phos., and Kali. Mur., alternately, both in the 6x or 3–200x potency, and at hourly intervals.

Give also Silicea in the 12x or 3–200x potency three doses a day.

Should the abscess, or boil, discharge and continue so without healing, change the remedies to Calc. Sulph., and Nat. Sulph., alternately, both at two-hourly intervals, using a 12x or 3–200x potency.

If, however, the discharge has become putrid and foul-smelling, give frequent doses of Kali. Phos., in a 3x or 3–200x potency.

Additional rest may be needed, and food which contains

plenty of fresh fruit and vegetables with sufficient assimilable iron, and vitamins B and C. (See chapters on these foods, pp. 78–83.)

Hot fomentations should be applied, and bathing the external parts with a solution of the remedies, using fresh lint at each application. To make this solution, use 3 doses of the remedy being given internally to half a cupful of hot water: the solution and the fomentation should be hot but reasonably comfortable for the patient.

Carbuncles: Use the same treatment as for Abscess, and Boils, and in addition take two doses daily of Calc. Fluor. in the 12x or the 3–200x potency.

Gangrene: If a condition seems like to become one of gangrene, or there is fear that this may be so, give Kali. Phos. in any potency available and preferably 12x or 3–200x, at frequent intervals: give also Kali. Sulph., Silicea, and Ferr. Phos., in the same potency in half-hourly doses.

BRONCHITIS: *Acute condition* with fever – Use Ferr. Phos., 6x or 3–200x, a dose every half-hour until the temperature has returned to normal.

All cases of bronchitis are likely to benefit from taking Ferr. Phos. since it carries oxygen to the lung tissues and assists in expelling morbid materials: except in the case of fever, as above, take a dose of Ferr. Phos. twice a day in a 12x or the 3–200x potency.

Chronic conditions: With a dry, painful cough – Use Nat. Mur., 12x[1] or 3–200x, three times a day, and the Ferr. Phos., as above, twice daily.

With loose, frothy phlegm – Use Nat. Mur., 12x[1] or 3–200x, three times a day, and the Ferr. Phos. as above, twice daily.

With thick and white or grey phlegm – Use Kali. Mur., 12x[1] or 3–200x, three times a day, and the Ferr. Phos. as above, twice daily.

[1] Young sufferers can use the 6x potency, four times a day. *All* elderly patients should also take a dose of Silicea each day, in a 12x or 3–200x potency to strengthen the bronchial walls.

Chronic bronchitis of some years' standing *may* need the prescription of Kali. Mur., or Kali. Sulph. to be supported with trace elements, to assist the debility of the weakened tissues.

All sufferers with bronchitis will need to see they are having sufficient vitamin A in their daily food. (See p. 75 for details of these requirements.)

Suitable massage can be of great benefit in chronic bronchitis. It increases the patient's strength and general nutrition, and exercises should be given, according to the age and strength of the sufferer, for improving the circulation and general mobility of the thorax. This treatment is to assist expectoration and respiration and act as a tonic to the lung tissues. The breathing exercises must especially help expiration. Abdominal massage should usually be included, unless there are contra-indications, and it is often of much benefit.

CATARRHS – NOSE AND THROAT: *Acute catarrh:* with thick, white phlegm, or these nasal exudations, use Kali. Mur., 3x or 3–200x, every hour till relieved.

Acute and heavy catarrh: With thick, yellow mucous, sometimes accompanied by picking of nose, give Nat. Phos., 6x or 3–200x, two or three doses at hourly intervals.

Chronic catarrh: Slight and watery: take Nat. Mur., and Calc. Phos., alternately, each twice a day, 12x or 3–200x potency.

If discharge is creamy-yellow, take Nat. Phos., 12x or 3–200x, twice a day before meals.

If the discharge is offensive, take Kali. Phos., and Silicea, alternately, 12x or 3–200x, each twice a day, between meals.

If mucous is greenish, use Nat. Sulph., 6x or 3–200x, at hourly intervals until it has altered – requiring another tissue remedy – or cleared.

Itching, or dryness of the edges or the tip of the nose, indicates a need for Silicea: use 12x or 3–200x, twice a day. If the nose is icy-cold at its extremity, take Calc. Phos., 12x or 3–200x, twice a day.

Catarrh of the Vagina: see *Leucorrhoea.*

CHILLS AND COLDS: If chilled, with shivering and cannot get warm, take Ferr. Phos., 3x or 3–200x: a dose every 15 minutes. And if possible, go to bed wrapped in a blanket, with a hot-water bottle.

Many chills are satisfactorily thrown off by taking a few doses of Ferr. Phos. only, but to be efficacious this remedy should be taken promptly.

At the first sign of having a cold – the throat is sore – take Ferr. Phos. 3x or 3–200x, frequently.

For a feverish cold, with a high temperature, take Ferr. Phos., 3x or 3–200x, approximately every half-hour while awake. A sleeper with a high temperature should not be wakened, but given the remedy on coming naturally out of sleep.

While the temperature is above normal, nothing should be eaten: a little cold water to drink, or fresh orange juice.

A blanket bath is advised: The patient, otherwise naked, is wrapped loosely in a blanket: a sponge or face flannel is immersed in cold/cool water and wrung almost dry. Within cover of the blanket lightly and quickly wipe the whole body with this flannel – first one side of the body, then the other, using a rolling action and adjusting the blanket. Then wrap closely with the blanket, and cover well with the usual eider-down and blankets. The patient may be expected to perspire freely and sleep. After several hours the patient will wake, feeling much better, and the temperature will be lower. It is not likely the temperature will go up and down: it will steadily come down.

When the temperature has returned to normal, 98·4°, or 99·0° at the very most, freshly made weak tea can be given, if desired. On returning to a normal temperature, and some patients go subnormal, a little bread and butter or toast should be given, preferably using brown bread to help the bowel action and provide the needed vitamin B. A few hours later, check for a steady temperature at normal and then light meals – using dairy produce, fruit and vegetables – can be resumed.

Watery stage of Colds, etc. – For watery running of nose, or eyes, or other part of the body, take Nat. Mur., 3x or 3–200x, hourly, with Ferr. Phos., every two hours in the same potency.

Mucous conditions – Where there is a clear, jelly-like mucous, or greyish-white phlegm, or a nasal exudation of similar description, take Kali. Mur., 6x or 3–200x, three doses daily.

If the mucous or phlegm is thick, and white or rather yellow, take Kali. Sulph., 12x or 3–200x, three times a day.

If the mucous is hard and knotty, take Silicea 12x, or 3–200x, three times a day.

For dryness at the back of the nose, take Nat. Mur., 3x or 3–200x, hourly.

For the sensation of stuffiness, or of being "stuffed up", take Kali. Mur., 12x or 3–200x, hourly.

If a *hacking cough* has developed, take Kali. Mur., 12x or 3–200x, four or five doses a day.

If the presence of phlegm causes *coughing*, but nothing is expelled, take Silicea, 12x or 3–200x, three or four times a day.

If spasms of *tickling cough* develop, take Mag. Phos., and Silicea alternately, 6x or 3–200x, during such spasms.

In all cases, frequently breathe OUT deeply.

CONSTIPATION: If the anus is dry and retentive, and all efforts at stool come to nothing, use Nat. Phos. at half-hourly intervals until the condition is easier and a bowel motion results: 6x or 3–200x potency.

If the bowel motion is difficult and dry, take Nat. Mur. for several days, a dose at bedtime and again in the morning, in the 6x or 3–200x potency.

If the bowel motion produces hard knotty stools, take Nat. Sulph. for several days, at bedtime and an early morning dose, in the 6x or 3–200x potency.

If there is no motion and the tongue is yellow, take Kali. Sulph., for several days, at bedtime and an early morning dose, in the 6x or 3–200x potency.

If the stools recede, with difficulty in expelling, take Calc. Fluor., and Silicea, a dose of each at bedtime and again in the early morning, 6x or 3–200x potency.

If there is no bowel action and the tongue is white, take Kali. Mur., for several days, a dose at bedtime and again in the morning, 6x or 3–200x potency.

If there is no desire to attend stool, take a dose each of Kali. Phos., and Calc. Fluor., at bedtime and again in the morning for several days, in the 12x or 3–200x potency.

If there seems to be inflammation, or heat, or pain in the bowel, take Ferr. Phos., every half-hour in the 6x or 3–200x potency, until the condition is relieved.

It is necessary to fix a time to attend stool as this assists in re-establishing satisfactory habits. Individuals vary in their needs as to whether this should be once, twice, or thrice daily.

In all cases of difficult bowel action, it is advisable to see that the meals contain enough vitamins, calcium and assimilable iron. (See pp. 57–84.)

It is *highly important for good health* that the bowels should show a healthy activity.

If the tissue remedies are taken as indicated for the various conditions of this trouble, natural and healthy motions should result within a short space of time. If the diet is deficient in its essential factors, referred to above, this should of course be adjusted at the same time. In some cases sufficient exercise may not be taken. In these circumstances a daily walk, or some indoor exercises and abdominal breathing should be undertaken.

Purgatives and laxatives containing medicinal paraffin oil are detrimental to the bowel and should not be used. Such measures interfere with intestinal absorption of vitamin and essential food products and weaken all natural bowel activities.

DEAFNESS: If this is accompanied by inflammation, giving heat and pain, or internal swelling localized close to the ear, give Ferr. Phos., alternated with Kali. Mur., in the 12x or 3–200x potency, in hourly doses of each, and then less frequently as the acute condition improves.

If the deafness is due primarily to a nervous cause, use Kali. Phos., and Mag. Phos., alternately, in the 12x or 3–200x potency, each every two hours, the Mag. Phos. is better taken in hot water.

If the deafness is worse in the evening, with noise in the head, accompanied by a slimy tongue and possibly yellowish exudation, give Kali. Sulph, in the 12x or 3–200x potency, evening doses at two-hourly intervals.

If there is hard matter in the ear, which causes the deafness, use Calc. Fluor., and Silicea alternately, in a 3x or 6x, or 3–200x potency, doses every 15 minutes. If these do not clear the condition within an hour or so, professional advice is needed.

General, chronic deafness; the chief remedies are Kali. Mur., Kali. Phos., Kali. Sulph., and Silicea, used alternately, in the 12x or 3–200x potency, or a 30x potency if the patient is elderly, two doses a day of each. Sufficient vitamins A and C need to be given in the daily meals. (See pp. 75 or 82.)

Deafness is sometimes occasioned by bone changes, when skilled professional advice may be of assistance.

DIARRHOEA: If the diarrhoea is giving greenish stools, take Nat. Sulph., hourly, in the 6x or 3–200x potency.

If the diarrhoea is giving stools containing blood and slime, take Kali. Mur., hourly, in the 6x or 3–200x potency.

If the diarrhoea is slimy, yellow, take Kali. Sulph., hourly, in the 6x or 3–200x potency.

If the diarrhoea is because of a chill, use Ferr. Phos. depending on this condition as to the dosage being taken (probably half-hourly), 3x or 6x, or 3–200x potency.

If the diarrhoea is foetid smelling, take Kali. Phos., 12x or 3–200x, three times a day.

If the diarrhoea contains frothy water, and is slimy, use Nat. Mur., 6x or 3–200x, hourly.

If the diarrhoea smells sour, is brown, liquid, and watery, use Nat. Phos., hourly, in the 6x or 3–200x potency.

If the diarrhoea shows undigested food, use Ferr. Phos., hourly, in the 12x or 3–200x potency.

FEMININE DISORDERS: *Dysmenorrhoea* (painful menstruation). Use Mag. Phos., and Calc. Fluor., alternately, both in the 6x or 3–200x potency: take hourly doses, with additional doses of Mag. Phos. in hot water for spasms of pain or for convulsive pain.

If the menstrual blood is dark and clotted, use Kali. Mur. instead of the Calc. Fluor., in the same potency and frequency of dose.

If the discharge during the latter part of the period becomes yellowish-brown, now use Kali. Sulph., in a 12x or 3–200x potency, three doses during the second half of each day.

For subjects who are soon nervously depleted, take three doses of Kali. Phos., each day towards the latter part of the period, and in the 12x or 3–200x potency.

Menorrhagia (heavy menstrual flow). Use Ferr. Phos., Calc. Phos., and Kali. Sulph., alternately: take three doses of each daily, in the 6x or 3–200x potency.

Dysmenorrhoea may be accompanied by an inability to relax, or by a deficiency of Calc. Fluor. in the glands, and the tissue remedies will quickly put this right: the *menorrhagia* indicates a mineral deficiency in the daily meals, notably of calcium and iron. (See also pp. 59 and 63 on these minerals.)

In both conditions where constipation is a factor, this of course needs attention. (See p. 92.)

If these measures have not established a normal and reasonably comfortable condition it is advisable to seek skilled advice.

Leucorrhoea (the "whites"). If the discharge is transparent and rather gelatinous use Calc. Phos. in the 6x or the 3–200x potency, and take three doses a day: if the discharge is white, take Kali. Mur. in the same potency, three times a day: if it is yellow in colour and stales to brown, take Kali. Sulph. in the same potency: if it is a golden creamy yellow take Nat. Phos., but if the discharge is watery, take Nat. Mur. In all cases the same potency and frequency of doses can be adhered to.

The condition is usually one of debility, sometimes of a catarrhal nature, and plenty of fresh air, some exercise, and sensible meals which include plenty of fresh vegetables, salads and fruit, are needed.

The Menopause. If the menopause brings digestive disturbance, or feelings of heaviness or sluggishness, take Nat. Phos., and Kali. Sulph., one dose of each during the morning and evening alternate days in the week; and more frequently if symptoms of an acid or irritating discharge are causing inconvenience or distress.

If flushings and hot waves occur, take Ferr. Phos. every ten minutes while these continue. A dose of Kali. Phos. is also advised.

If nervously inclined, take a dose of Kali. Phos. each day until this condition has improved.

A potency of 6x or 3–200x is suitable in all these remedies for the above conditions.

If there should be occasional periods of menorrhagia, use the remedies as given for this condition.

Plenty of fresh air, a daily walk, some good breathing exercises, light food which contains an adequate intake of assimilable iron and vitamins, and freedom from anxiety, these measures should ensure a natural, easy development from one period of life to the next.

FEVERS: *High Fevers* – symptoms of fever with high temperature – use Ferr. Phos. every fifteen minutes until the temperature gradually drops, lessening the frequency of the dose to hourly and two-hourly intervals. A 6x potency will ordinarily be used, but if the condition gives 102° or more, (except in a child) a 30x potency will be needed. Children easily run a high temperature, and the 6x potency in their case should be correct.

If the Ferr. Phos. does not suffice to bring the temperature down gradually, and particularly if the sufferer has a highly nervous temperament, give Kali. Phos. in a 3x potency. As soon as there is an improvement, alternate the Ferr. Phos. with the Kali. Phos.

(If the 3–200x potency is being used, the one potency is given of both the remedies in all circumstances.)

If, subsequently, the fever is under control but the temperature rises in the evening to any degree, give then Kali. Sulph., 6x or 3–200x, in two doses of two-hourly intervals.

A gentle but quick sponge-over with a flannel or sponge squeezed out of cold/tepid water while the sufferer is between blankets assists the control of the temperature and is a relief to the patient. Wrap the blankets rounds the patient afterwards and cover suitably.

If the bowel is *temporarily* inactive in feverish chills, after about thirty-six hours Nat. Mur. should be given. (See treatment for Constipation, p. 92.)

Low Fevers – with symptoms of severe chilling, cannot get warm, subnormal temperature, nausea or vertigo, intermittent and bilious fever, chilling with vomiting or diarrhoea, influenza with gripe.

Give Nat. Sulph., and Kali. Phos., in the 3x or the 3–200x potency, both in half-hourly doses until the temperature is normal, the sickness, vertigo, and gripe have lessened: if the temperature then runs high, give Ferr. Phos., in the 6x or 3–200x potency.

When the acute stage has passed, give these three remedies, preferably in a 6x or 12x, or 3–200x, potency, each three times a day.

Specific Fevers (alphabetically arranged):

Brain Fever, with delirium. Use Ferr. Phos., and Kali. Phos.,

D

alternately, a dose of each remedy at approximately half-hourly intervals, in the 12x or the 3–200x potency, and Nat. Mur., in the same potency, every two hours.

Chickenpox (Infectious).[1] Give Ferr. Phos., Kali. Mur., and Nat. Mur., in alternate doses throughout the illness, in a 6x or 3–200x potency: unless very severe give a dose of each remedy every two hours for the first two days, and then three times a day.

Diphtheria (characterized by grave throat symptoms and the formation of patches of congestion on mucous surfaces, highly infectious). For the slight fever, the stiffness of the neck, and the swelling of the glands at the jaw angle, give Ferr. Phos., Kali. Mur., and Nat. Phos. alternately, each remedy every two hours, in the 12x or the 3–200x potency. In addition, use all three remedies as a compound gargle, several times daily.

If there is exhaustion, give Kali. Phos., in a 3x, or 6x, or 3–200x potency, in half-hourly doses until there is an improvement.

If the patches of congestion on the throat spread, forming a membrane down the larynx causing difficulty in breathing, give Kali. Mur. alternately with Calc. Phos., in the 12x, 30x, or 3–200x potency, every half-hour.

If watery diarrhoea or vomit is present during the illness, give Nat. Mur. in a 12x or 3–200x potency, hourly until the condition has improved.

Similarly, if greenish watery diarrhoea or vomit is present give Nat. Sulph. in the same potency and frequency until this condition has improved.

A cautious and protracted convalescence is necessary. Any constipation will need attention. (See specific treatment p. 93.)

Glandular Fever (Infectious). Sudden stiffness of the neck, inability or difficulty in swallowing, and fever. After three days the cervical glands become enlarged and tender; debility

---

[1] Note differential diagnosis with Smallpox. (The rash consists of small rose-spots, which become raised vesicles in 24 hours: appears first on neck and chest, and spreads over entire body in crops.)

and constipation. (See treatment for Constipation.) The glands do not suppurate; convalescence is often slow.

For the fever give Ferr. Phos., in the 6x or 3–200x potency, probably every hour, unless the fever should become sharp and run high, when more frequent doses will control it: give less frequent doses as soon as the fever is down to 100° or 101°. As soon as the glands become swollen, give Kali. Mur., in the 6x or 3–200x potency, every two hours.

The bowels should be kept active, and the patient should rest in bed. A light, nourishing diet is suitable as soon as the temperature has become normal. When the swelling of the glands has subsided, change from Kali. Mur., and give Calc. Phos., and Ferr. Phos., alternately, in the 12x or 3–200x potency, three doses of each daily, to assist the convalescence.

Hay Fever, Sinusitis: Acute – Use Ferr. Phos., and Nat. Mur. alternately in the 3x or the 3–200x potency, half-hourly until relieved.

Chronic – Use Nat. Mur., Silicea, Kali. Phos., each two-hourly in alternation, for two days, and then twice daily, in the 12x or 3–200x potency.

In severe cases a compound prescription which has included trace elements has proved effective.

Skilled manipulative treatment is generally of considerable benefit, particularly if given with these remedies.

Influenza: The "Ache" – Where there is an aching all over, take Nat. Sulph., 3x or 3–200x, every half-hour. This should break up the aching.

If chilled, use also Ferr. Phos., alternately, 3x or 3–200x.

Fever – If the temperature rises, leave the Nat. Sulph., and take only Ferr. Phos., 3x or 3–200x, every half-hour. If possible, go to bed, wrapped in a blanket, and have the treatment as for a feverish chill with a blanket bath.

Have *nothing to eat until* the temperature has dropped to normal: drink cold water or fresh orange juice.

This is the normal and safe way to get well quickly.

If there is much wateriness from the nose, the eyes, etc., use Nat. Mur., 3x or 3–200x, every two or three hours.

Use Kali. Mur., and Kali. Sulph. alternately for the convalescent aches and tiredness and drained feeling: 12x or 3–200x, each twice a day, and a dose of Kali. Phos., 12x, at bedtime.

Gastric conditions – If at the commencement of the illness, gastric symptoms are predominant, take Nat. Sulph., and Nat. Phos., alternately, 3x or 3–200x, each every half-hour, and less frequently as the condition improves.

If gastric symptoms (pain, nausea) continue in some degree throughout the illness, take one dose each of Nat. Sulph. and Nat. Phos., at night and in the morning, using 12x or 3–200x potency.

Measles. (Infectious.) Symptoms: sudden fever, running at the nose and eyes; rash on the fourth day on forehead and face, with increased fever for about a week.

Give Ferr. Phos., Kali. Mur., and Kali. Sulph. Use the Ferr. Phos. while there is fever, and also if the temperature should rise again when the rash appears. (With these remedies this will most probably be slight.) Use the 6x or the 3–200x potency as in high fever.

If wateriness of the nose and eyes is present, give Nat. Mur., at two-hourly intervals, and the same potency.

If the cough or catarrh develops, use the Kali. Mur., and do so after the rash has appeared and developed: give three or four doses a day in the 6x or 3–200x potency.

When all signs of fever have subsided and the rash has faded, give Kali. Sulph. to clear the subsequent skin condition, in the same potency, three times a day. The Ferr. Phos. should not now be needed.

If at any time during the illness catarrhal diarrhoea is present with green offensive stools, give two or three doses of Nat. Sulph. in the 6x or 3–200x potency, at two-hourly intervals.

If constipation is present, see treatment under this heading.

Mumps. (Infectious before the glands are affected and for two to three weeks after.) Symptoms: pain under one ear with stiffness or soreness of neck and jaw, with fever, usually

101°–103° or more: swelling of the parotid gland, which is tender and elastic to pressure: mastication and swallowing are very painful, foul breath, furred tongue. Both sides of the neck may be involved and the swelling form a collar, or first one side is affected and then the other. As soon as the swelling subsides there is rapid improvement: the glands rarely suppurate.

The bowels should be kept active from the beginning of the illness. (See treatment for Constipation.) An antiseptic mouth-wash is helpful, and hot fomentations should be applied to the swellings. Male patients need to be kept in bed for about ten days, against the possible risk of orchitis.

Between the fomentations, a light scarf should be worn to keep the affected parts warm. (Do not give hot fomentations while the fever is running.)

Give Ferr. Phos. for the fever in the 6x or 3–200x potency, every half-hour while this is acute and then less frequently as soon as it is under control. As soon as the swelling appears, give Kali. Mur., 6x or 3–200x, four doses daily, alternately with Nat. Mur., in the same potency, until all pain, stiffness, and swelling have gone, and the tongue is normal.

If the fever should run very high, a blanket bath should prove a relief to the sufferer. (See treatment of High Fever, p. 96.)

Rheumatic Fever. Symptoms: the temperature is moderately high with general soreness and stiffness, and then rheumatic pain in one of the larger joints. The affected joint is red, hot, swollen, with much pain: later the redness subsides and the joint becomes dead-white in appearance. There is marked sweating with a sourish smell: the tongue is large, flat, and thickly furred. The urine is scanty and highly coloured.

Give Ferr. Phos., and Nat. Phos., alternately, in the 6x or 3–200x potency, both remedies at half-hourly intervals and less frequently as the fever subsides and the condition improves.

For the sharp, shooting pains use Mag. Phos., in the same potency and in hot water, also half-hourly until these have subsided. If there is local swelling around joints, use Kali. Mur., and Nat. Phos., alternately, in a 12x or 3–200x potency, and at two-hourly intervals. If, however, there are watery symptoms, use instead Nat. Mur., and Nat. Phos., in the 12x or 3–200x potency and at two-hourly intervals. If the pains move about from one place to another, use instead Kali. Sulph., in the 12x or 3–200x potency and at two-hourly intervals.

Scarlet Fever (Infectious). The symptoms are vomiting, pains in the back and limbs, sore throat, high fever and headache, rapid pulse: the glands at the jaw angle swell: a rash shows on the chest and then spreads over the face and body.

If the temperature is high give Ferr. Phos., in the 12x or 3–200x potency, half-hourly: also give Kali. Mur., in the 12x or 3–200x potency at two-hourly intervals, with Kali. Sulph. in the same potency in the evening at two-hourly intervals.

The Kali. Sulph. promotes the needed development of the rash and the subsequent peeling of the skin; and it is given to cure any dropsy that may be present.

If there should be stupor or extreme exhaustion during the illness, give Kali. Phos. in the 12x or 3–200x potency; also if the throat becomes sore *and putrid*. In these circumstances the doses can be inserted inside the lower lip: repeat half-hourly until the condition has improved.

While the temperature is high no food should be given, only cold water or the juice from a squeezed orange to drink.

Throughout this illness all *protein* food should only be given in minimum quantities to relieve the strain on the kidneys.

Give a daily toilet with tepid sponging, and if the bowels are inactive give the indicated remedies. (See treatment for Constipation p. 93.)

If the illness is slight or aborted, the symptoms will be slight and may escape notice except for later skin eruptions or some nephritis.

Smallpox (Highly infectious). There may be shivering, frontal headache, vomiting, pains in the back, temperature runs up. The rash appears on the third day of fever on the face, forehead, and scalp, and spreads to the wrists, the trunk, arms, and legs, at first as red raised papules: three days later these become vesicles.

For the high temperature give Ferr. Phos. in the 12x or 3–200x potency, frequently: give also Kali. Mur. in the 12x or 3–200x potency, hourly. If, after the rash and papules have appeared the temperature runs high, give Kali. Phos., in a 12x, 30x, or 3–200x potency, since this is a secondary condition with a septic type of fever: give hourly and then two-hourly doses.

Give daily tepid sponging, and cold compresses to the eyes: exclude the light from windows.

On the papules becoming purulent,[1] give alternate doses of Kali. Phos., and Nat. Sulph., in the 12x or 3–200x potency, both remedies four times a day.

Mild forms may be confused with chickenpox.

Distinguishing features of the smallpox rash, not present in chickenpox: The papules are indented or divided. Inflammation surrounds the vesicles.

The rash appears on the third day: in chickenpox it develops on the first day.

The fever declines as soon as the eruptions appear: this is not so in chickenpox.

If on the eighth day the vesicles become purulent, there is much inflammation and swelling and later disfigurement.

Tonsillitis. For the hot, dry throat and high temperature give Ferr. Phos. internally and as a gargle. Use a 6x potency, or the 3–200x, and give a dose every half-hour, and then hourly as soon as there is an improvement. For the gargle dissolve three or four doses in half a cup of warm water. Give a cold compress to the frontal headache.

See that the bowels are acting freely, and keep them so during the illness. (See treatment for Constipation p. 93.)

[1] Containing pus.

As the illness develops, for the enlarged glands and swollen tissues give Kali. Mur., and Nat. Phos., alternately, in a 12x or 3–200x potency, three or four doses of each a day, and now only one or two doses a day of the Ferr. Phos. If there is difficulty, now, in using a gargle the throat can be sprayed with the Kali. Mur., made up as a gargle, which is excellent for this purpose.

If *Quinsies* develop: Give Silicea, in the 12x or 3–200x potency, three doses a day.

During convalescence the meals need to contain foods rich in calcium, iron, and the vitamins.

There may be difficulty in diagnosis in distinguishing between acute tonsillitis and diphtheria. In tonsillitis the fever is generally high, with the throat also hot, and the headache is severe: in diphtheria the fever symptoms are generally slight.

Typhoid or Typhus. (Infections.) Intense headache, nausea, temperature rapidly runs up, vomiting, rigors and pains all over the body, the pupils are contracted, tongue thickly furred, constipation, exhaustion, noisy delirium, eyes and face suffused: rash on the fifth day beginning on the abdomen, the upper part of the chest, hands and wrists, and later the rest of the body.

For the continuous high fever give Kali. Phos. in a high potency, 12x, or 30x, or 3–200x, every hour, or every two hours if the sufferer is elderly: give also Calc. Phos. in the same potency twice a day.

If fluid is present in the tissues give Nat. Mur., in a 12x or 3–200x potency, two or three doses a day.

If a rash has developed, give Kali. Sulph., in a 12x potency, or the 3–200x, three doses a day.

Throughout the illness an evening dose of Kali. Sulph. is advised in the 12x or 3–200x potency.

If constipation is present, for treatment, see under Constipation.

FIBROSITIS (treat as for chronic rheumatism). Take one dose of silicea daily, 12x, or 3–200x.

Use Ferr. Phos. 6x or 3–200x, for any acute inflammatory conditions – heat, swelling, and pain in any part of the body – at hourly intervals until the condition is easier.

In damp weather, one dose of Nat. Sulph. is also of benefit: 6x or 3–200x.

Skilled manipulative treatment is of great benefit, also, if this is available.

If an inflammatory condition persists, this sometimes happens in the trapezius or the intercostals, use Kali. Phos. rather than Ferr. Phos., to deal with the toxic condition which has localized, and is causing the inflammation. Breath-ing-*out* exercises are advised to assist in clearing some probable congestion of the liver, and to improve the digestion by the elimination of used carbonic acid gas from the tissues.

INJURIES (alphabetically arranged):

Immediate Injuries. To mitigate shock and bleeding, give at once Kali. Phos., and Ferr. Phos., together, in a little water or dissolved in one's own saliva: introduce the solution or thin paste inside the lower lip or on to the tongue of the injured person. Frequent doses at ten-minute intervals, and then less frequently as needed, using any potency rather than none, but preferably 3x, or 6x, or 3–200x.

Neglected Injuries. If festering, use Silicea, 6x or 3–200x, but if continuing sanious use Calc. Sulph. instead in the same potency, using these remedies three times a day until easier.

Bites and Stings. Take internally Nat. Mur., 3x, or 6x, or 3–200x: also Silicea and Kali. Phos., if severe, in the same potency. Doses every ten minutes. For subsequent swelling use Kali. Mur., instead of Nat. Mur., in the 12x or 3–200x potency if available, three or four doses a day. *Also*, use these remedies as a lotion in paste form, with the saliva. The Kali. Phos. has an antiseptic quality. Renew the lotion as it dries off.

Bleeding and Cuts. Take Ferr. Phos. internally at ten-minute intervals, until bleeding subsides. If parts swell, then use Kali. Mur., three or four doses a day, lessening doses as the condition improves. If parts are torn or lacerated, use also Kali. Phos.

The dressing should be soaked also in a solution of Ferr. Phos., together with the Kali. Phos. if it is being used. Bandage well over this dressing. The solution can be renewed through the dressing without removing this.

Nose-bleed. Use Ferr. Phos., and Kali. Phos., taken internally at ten-minute intervals until bleeding has stopped, in the 3x, 6x, or 3–200x potency. If, however, the bleeding is black and clotted, use instead Kali. Mur., at similar intervals and in the same potency.

Blood poisoning. Use Nat. Mur. and Kali. Phos., internally, 12x or 3–200x, probably four times a day, as needed: use these remedies also as a solution on a dressing where practicable.

Bruises (flesh). Use Ferr. Phos. for the inflammation, and Kali. Mur. for any swelling, in potency of 3x, or 6x, or 3–200x, taken internally at ten-minute intervals until easier, and subsequently two or three times a day if still necessary.

Use the same remedies as a cool lotion with a lint dressing under a bandage.

Bruises of the shin ribs, etc. (bones). Use a lotion of Calc. Fluor. on lint under a bandage or suitable dressing.

Burns and Scalds. Use Ferr. Phos. and Kali Mur. internally, at ten-minute intervals, 3x or 3–200x. A solution of Kali. Mur. on lint can be given to prevent blistering. For this purpose do not remove a lint dressing, but add the lotion to the lint and cover with another piece of lint. It is now recognized, however, that these injuries are generally better kept as dry as possible.

Kali. Phos. should also be given for shock, internally, 3x or 3–200x, at suitable intervals as for an acute condition.

Head injuries – falls, blows, concussion. Use Ferr. Phos., and Nat. Sulph., internally, inserted as a thin wet paste with the saliva into the mouth or inside the lower lip, using 3x or 3–200x: repeat at fifteen-minute intervals until the condition has improved: if the concussion is serious and gives little response give the doses three or four times over the twenty-four hours, and use a higher potency.

Treat any external bruises or cuts with the indicated remedies under these categories.

Hernia and rupture. Take Calc. Fluor., and Silicea, alternately, in the 6x or 3–200x potency. Apply a cold compress over the swelling, and preferably soaked first in a solution of Calc. Fluor. Keep the knees raised.

Patella (Knee-cap). Injured by falling. Use Calc. Fluor. in the 6x or 3–200x potency, internally, and as a lotion on lint: dose and applications every thirty minutes until the condition is easier, and then two or three times a day, preferably in a higher potency. Rest the leg with a cushion under the knee to keep it slightly flexed.

In the case of a fracture, this will need to be set.

Sprains – with inflammation; use Ferr. Phos., internally and as a lotion, in the 6x or 3–200x potency, internally every ten minutes to commence with, and then hourly: renew the lotion as it dries off.

For the swelling, change from Ferr. Phos. to Kali. Mur., in the same potency, both internally and as a lotion, at hourly intervals.

Rest the injured part.

Strains. Take Kali Mur., and Calc. Fluor., alternately, in the 6x or 3–200x potency, at hourly and then two-hourly intervals.

Rest the injured part.

Sunstroke. Give Nat. Mur. dissolved as a paste with the saliva: place on tongue or inside lower lip, with a cold water compress against the *top* of the head and across the forehead.

INSOMNIA. If the sleeplessness is *occasional*, or *intermittent* – and if from working late in the evening, from worry, or excitement (nervous causes), take Kali. Phos., 30x, or 3–200x, about an hour before retiring, on getting into bed, and should this be necessary, another dose one hour later if still awake.

If from a feeling of pressure of blood to the head (congestive) take Ferr. Phos., in the 30x or 3–200x potency, and at intervals as given above.

If with stomach discomfort, or with symptoms of acidity (digestive) – heartburn, creamy tongue, creamy exudation at the corners of the eyes – take Nat. Phos., 6x or 3–200x, at intervals as given above.

If the sleeplessness is *persistent*, and the above remedies do not suffice, it is probable a trace element is needed in the prescription. There may also be over-fatigue and a need for more exercise and fresh air than is being obtained, particularly towards the end of the day. The meals should contain sufficient vitamin and mineral intake. Skilled manipulation of the neck and head tissues is of value in relieving congestion and improving the circulation to the brain.

If the sleeplessness is caused by weakness of the heart muscle, and indicated by hearing the heart beat when lying on the left side, take Calc. Fluor., Kali. Phos., and Nat. Mur., in the 12x or the 3–200x potency, one dose of each remedy at bedtime and again in the morning until the condition has improved.

LUMBAGO *from chill*. Take Ferr. Phos., in the 6x or 3–200x potency, frequently, with alternate doses of Kali. Mur., in the 3x or 3–200x potency, and Nat. Phos., in the 6x or 3–200x potency: each remedy will need to be taken hourly. A hot-water bottle against the affected part is a comfort.

Suddenly, from strain with much pain and binding of muscles. Take Calc. Fluor., Mag. Phos., and Calc. Phos., in the 6x or 3–200x potency, every twenty minutes for the first two hours, and then a dose of each remedy once every two hours. The Mag. Phos. is best taken in hot water, and if the 3–200x potency is used take three times the ordinary dose each time.

If skilled manipulative treatment is available, this usually puts the matter right very quickly.

NASAL CONDITIONS. Itching, or dryness of the edges or the tip of the nose indicates a need for Silicea: use 12x, or 3–200x, twice a day.

If the nose is icy-cold at its extremity, take Calc. Phos., 12x or 3–200x, twice a day.

Offensive discharge. Give Kali. Phos., 3x or 3–200x, hourly. (In nervous subjects nose-bleed may also occur, or frequent sneezing.)

Persistent sneezing (with chill). Use Ferr. Phos., and Nat. Mur. alternately, 3x or 3–200x, every half hour until eased.

Polypus. Take Calc. Phos., 3x or 3–200x, three doses a day. See also that the daily vitamin D intake is adequate: a vitamin supplement may be necessary. Every opportunity should be taken for sensible exposure to the sun's rays.

Sense of Smell. If lost, try Mag. Phos., 12x or 3–200x. If diminished, use Kali. Sulph., Silicea, and Mag. Phos., alternately, each three times a day in the 3x or 3–200x potency.

Sense of Stuffiness. Use Kali. Mur., 3x or 3–200x, four times during the day, or night.

Ulcerations. Inside the nose, surface ulceration, in children, give Calc. Phos., 3x, three doses a day.

Deep ulceration, in adults, discharge corrodes, give Silicea, 12x or 3–200x, three times a day: syringe, or bathe, with a solution of same in warm water.

NERVOUS DISORDERS. *Nervous depression:* Take Kali. Phos., in the 3x or 3-200x potency, at hourly intervals.

Hysteria: Give Kali. Phos., in the 3x or 3-200x potency, every ten minutes.

Nervous exhaustion, with irritability: Take Kali. Phos., and Nat. Phos., in the 3x or 3–200x potency, every ten minutes.

Obsessions: Neurosis: Mania: Give Kali. Phos., Mag. Phos., and Nat. Phos., three doses of each daily, in the 12x or 3–200x potency, and one dose of Silicea daily in the 12x or 3–200x potency.

Nervous shock: Give Kali. Phos., and Mag. Phos., in the 6x or 3–200x potency, frequently for immediate treatment: three times a day in the 12x or 3–200x potency for prolonged conditions, and for delayed nervous shock, with a dose of Silicea once a day in the same potency.

If the condition is accompanied by constipation, try giving Nat. Mur. twice a day in the same potency, and increase the intake of vitamin B foods in the meals.

Nervous vertigo: Take Kali. Phos., in the 3x or 3–200x potency, but if with biliousness, take Nat. Sulph. instead in the same potency: frequent doses until normal.

Sea and travel sickness: Take Nat. Phos., and Kali. Phos., in the 12x or 3–200x potency, two doses before starting and during the travel: at half-hourly intervals if the condition becomes acute: but at two-hourly intervals as a preventive.

This procedure has been found excellent.

Trembling, shaking, or giddiness from inside oneself: Take Kali. Phos., Ferr. Phos., and Mag. Phos., in the 3x or 3–200x potency, two doses of each within a few minutes of each: continue further doses if these should be necessary.

Where there is hesitancy and shrinking from work from nervous debility, or from nervous shock: Take Kali. Phos., once a day, and Ferr. Phos., and Silicea three times a day, in the 12x or 3–200x potency. See that the meals really contain sufficient mineral and vitamin content. (Refer to this section, pp. 57–84.)

NEURITIS. Take Ferr. Phos., and Kali. Phos., alternately. If the condition has come on suddenly and is acute, the 3x or the 3–200x potency should be used every fifteen minutes, then half-hourly, and each remedy every two hours as soon as the pain has lessened.

If there are pressure points on the nerve from rheumatism in a neighbouring joint (usually the shoulder), or the humerus is out of alignment with pressure on the nerve and limitation of movement of the arm, these are indications that skilled manipulation and suitable massage is required.

The addition of Nat. Phos. in a 12x or 3–200x potency, several doses daily, will assist in clearing any rheumatic congestion present.

PILES (or Haemorrhoids). With low back pains, constipation and itching, take Calc. Fluor., in the 12x or 3–200x potency: use also as a lotion.

If bleeding with bright blood, use Ferr. Phos., in the 12x or 3–200x potency: use also as a lotion.

If bleeding with dark clotted blood, use Kali. Mur., in the 6x or 3–200x potency, and as a lotion.

If there are sharp darting pains, use Mag. Phos., in the 6x or 3–200x potency.

If the Piles are accompanied by a feeling of heat in the descending colon or rectum, take Nat. Sulph. in the 12x or 3–200x potency.

If the condition is acute, take half-hourly and hourly doses; if chronic, three and four doses a day are advised.

If the condition is a general one, see that the meals contain sufficient calcium and iron, see these sections pp. 59–68, and if constipation is a feature or the daily movements need assistance, see the section on Constipation, pp. 92–93.

SCIATICA. An excruciating pain along the course of the sciatic nerve, running from under the buttocks to the knee. Take Kali. Phos., 3x or 3–200x, every fifteen minutes, half-hourly and hourly as the condition improves. If the pain is shooting, with spasms, take also Mag. Phos. in the same potency, preferably in hot water.

If there is some contraction of the muscles of the affected leg, take also Nat. Mur. in the same potency.

If accompanied by Rheumatism, take several doses of Nat. Phos., in the 3x potency if this is acute and in a higher potency or the 3–200x if this is a constitutional tendency.

If the Sciatica proves obstinate, take Silicea, Ferr. Phos., and Calc. Phos., alternately, three times a day, each in the 12x or 3–200x potency.

(*Note:* The bowels should be active, and in obstinate conditions there may be pelvic congestion needing specific attention.)

SKIN DISORDERS: *Acne and Pimples* – with inflammation of the skin, take Ferr. Phos., and Nat. Phos., 3x or 3–200x potency; if with hard matter, take Calc. Phos. and Silicea in the 3x or 3–200x potency.

If the Acne is slow to heal, remaining moist and yellow, take Nat. Sulph., in the 3x or the 3–200x potency.

If young peo ple, also give Calc. Phos., in a 3x, or 6x, or 3–200x potency

In each case, three doses a day.

(*Note:* See that the meals contain a good content of calcium foods, assimilable iron, and vitamin C, see pp. 59–80.)

Alopecia. The chief remedy is Kali. Phos., in a 12x or 3–200x potency, three doses a day, with rest from nervous worry.

Other remedies may be needed constitutionally, in support – Nat. Mur., or Kali. Sulph., in a 12x or 3–200x potency, one or two doses a day.

Corns. Take Kali. Mur., and Silicea, both remedies in a 3–200x potency, three times a day.

If these are on the feet, bathe the feet daily, change the hosiery frequently, and have well-fitting shoes: exercises for the feet, a few minutes twice or thrice a day without the shoes on are in any case helpful for improving the circulation and the condition of the feet.

Chaps and Cracks of the skin. Nat. Mur. and Calc. Fluor. should be taken, in the 12x or 3–200x potency, three doses of each every day for a short period.

Dandruff and dryness. Take Kali. Sulph., and Nat. Mur., in a 12x or 3–200x potency, two doses of each every day for a period of two to three weeks.

Eczema – after vaccinations: Take Kali. Mur.; if eruptions are watery, use Nat. Mur.; but if these have yellow, watery secretions use Nat. Phos., and Nat. Sulph., alternately.

If the eruption brings irritation, take Kali. Phos., and Nat.

Phos., but if there is redness with burning pain take Ferr. Phos. and Nat. Phos.

In all these conditions a 12x or the 3–200x potency is advised, three doses a day.

Inflammation (and redness) The first remedy for any inflammation of the skin is Kali. Mur. Take frequent doses of the 6x or 3–200x potency.

Ringworm on body or scalp: Give Kali. Mur., Kali. Sulph., Nat. Phos., and Silicea, in the 6x or 3–200x potency, three doses of each every day.

Shingles, or Herpes. Take Kali. Phos., and Nat. Mur., alternately, each three times a day in the 6x or 3–200x potency. If the temperature usually registers as subnormal, add a dose each day of Nat. Sulph., preferably in the 12x or 3–200x potency.

Two doses each day of Calc. Phos., and of Ferr. Phos., should be taken also as a tonic in the 3–200x potency.

(*Note:* The meals should be rich in calcium and assimilable iron foods, and in vitamins B and C: refer, please, to these sections.)

Warts. Take Kali. Mur., and Silicea alternately, in the 3–200x potency, three times a day: add Nat. Sulph., in this potency, twice a day if the constitution is a bilious one.

STOMACH DISORDERS. *Acidity.* Take Nat. Phos., in the 3x or 3–200x potency, frequently, and a daily dose of Ferr. Phos., in the 12x or 3–200x potency.

(See that the meals contain sufficient assimilable iron in the foods chosen.)

Biliousness. Rest from food. Take Nat. Sulph. in the 3x potency frequently: twenty-four hours later fresh weak tea and dry biscuits (Vita-wheat, digestive, or home-made) are usually suitable; and Kali. Mur., in the 6x or 3–200x potency, three doses a day, with Nat. Sulph., in the 12x or 3–200x potency, one dose a day.

Gastritis. Rest from food. Take Ferr. Phos., and Kali. Mur., alternately, in the 6x or 3–200x potency, both remedies hourly; and for the nervous exhaustion take Kali. Phos., in the same potency, at two-hourly intervals.

Heartburn. Usually needs Ferr. Phos., and Nat. Phos., alternately, in the 6x or 3–200x potency, frequent doses.

Bilious conditions, however, will probably need alternate doses of Nat. Mur., Nat. Sulph., and Silicea, frequent doses in the same potency.

Rest from all food for a short period until the condition is cured.

Ulceration of Stomach. Take Kali. Phos., and Nat. Phos., in the 3x or the 3–200x potency, at half-hourly intervals and within five minutes of the first remedy for acute conditions. Take two-hourly doses for chronic conditions.

It is usually advisable to feed those with this condition with milk, and purées of fruit and vegetables, until the condition has healed.

Worry and anxiety need to be resolved to obtain the best and lasting results.

(A fasting régime is likely to produce anxiety and is not considered suitable for this condition.)

Indigestion (Dyspepsia: Gastric disorder). Stomach tender, red tongue, vomit shows undigested food: take Ferr. Phos., in the 6x or 3–200x potency, half-hourly, and rest from all food; drink cold water in sips.

If there is flatulence, with sharp spasms or cramp in the stomach, take Mag. Phos., in hot water, 3x, or three doses at once of the 3–200x: repeat at frequent intervals while the condition lasts.

If there is excessive flatulence with heart discomfort and pain, take Calc. Fluor., and Kali. Phos., alternately, in the 3x or 3–200x potency, at frequent intervals while the condition lasts.

If the tongue is greyish-white, sometimes with pain under the right shoulder, take Kali. Mur., in the 6x or the 3–200x potency, at hourly intervals: if this does not shortly improve the condition, take also Calc. Sulph. in the same potency, five minutes after the dose of Kali. Mur.

If the indigestion comes from a sense of fullness, usually worse in the evening, take a dose of Kali. Sulph., in the early afternoon and early evening, in the 12x or 3–200x potency.

If there is discomfort after eating fat, or starches, take Kali. Mur., in the 6x or 3–200x potency, three doses at hourly intervals, and reduce the intake of these foods.

If there is a bitter taste after taking food, rest from eating and take several doses of Nat. Sulph., in the 3x or the 3–200x potency, at hourly intervals.

URINATION. *Retention* – Take Mag. Phos. in hot water, in the 3x or the 3–200x potency, frequently until the condition is normal. This is generally from nervous causes or direct suppression.

In children it is probably from chill, and Ferr. Phos. should be given in the 3x or 3–200x potency, frequently until normal.

Frequent or copious – Take Nat. Mur., and Nat. Phos., alternately in the 12x or 3–200x potency, twice a day.

Scalding – Take Ferr. Phos., and Kali. Phos., alternately, in a 6x or 3–200x potency, three doses a day.

Burning – Take Ferr. Phos., and Nat. Mur., alternately, in a 6x or 3–200x potency, three doses a day.

Interrupted, with inflammation – Take Ferr. Phos., Kali. Mur., Nat. Sulph., three doses of each daily, in the 12x or 3–200x potency.

Very painful, accompanied by the passing of mucous, pus, blood – Take Kali. Phos., Silicea, and seek specialized advice. These remedies will probably be needed in a 12x potency, three times a day.

Incontinence. From weakness of muscles – Take Ferr. Phos., in a 12x or 3–200x potency, three times a day.

From weakness of nerve – Take Kali. Phos., in a 12x or 3–200x potency, three times a day.

In children – Give Nat. Phos., and Kali. Phos., a dose of each in the 3x or the 3–200x potency, three times a day, until the condition is normal.

Worms. If this condition is suspected, use Nat. Mur., and Nat. Phos. in alternation, in the 3–200x potency, four doses of each daily.

Thread-worms – Use Nat. Phos., 3x, and give an anal injection of four doses of Nat. Mur., 3x, dissolved in a small teacupful of warm water.

Others – Use Nat. Mur., in a 12x or 3–200x potency, four doses a day, and Nat. Phos. and Silicea, in a 12x or 3–200x potency, twice a day.

Pain is often of composite character. Treat first its major factor, i.e. soreness, or shooting pain, or dull ache, etc. The following guide gives the relative Tissue Salts for reducing painful conditions. (Dosage: half-hourly for acute conditions and then less often.)

Pain allied to swellings:	*use*	Kali. Mur.
because of strains, hernias:		Ferr. Phos., & Calc. Fluor.
colic and/or flatulence:		Mag. Phos.
cramp:		Calc. Phos. & Mag. Phos.
gastric pain and gripe:		Nat. Phos., Mag. Phos., & Nat. Sulph.
headaches:		
cervical, back of head:		Kali. Sulph., Kali. Mur., & Ferr. Phos.
frontal:		Kali. Phos. & Mag. Phos.
neck, shoulders, stiff or sting:		*see* fibrositis.
indigestion:		Nat. Phos. & Mag. Phos.
irritation of and under skin:		*see* skin disorders—shingles.
menstrual, or muscle pains—dull aching:		Kali. Mur.
"pins and needles", numbness, with heaviness, stiffness:		Kali. Phos.
soreness, throbbing:		Ferr. Phos.
under shoulder blades or at points of shoulders:		Kali. Mur.

(When in pain, it is generally advisable to feed lightly to assist clearance of the liver.)

Appendix

Trace Elements

SOME sufferers with rheumatic and arthritic conditions will need compound prescriptions of biochemic nutrients which incorporate certain trace elements. These trace elements have a special relationship to the main constituents of the prescription and function as catalysts and synergists in achieving the required chemical processes of regeneration.

Advanced conditions are likely to need these compound prescriptions.[1]

How to Understand Rheumatism and Arthritis

Rheumatism and arthritis are classed as diseases of metabolism – as distinct from virus infections.

The pains of rheumatism are felt in muscle tissues, in tendons, and in inflammatory conditions of the joints: arthritis is an allied disease of the joints and the bones.

The cells and the intercellular fluids of the body depend upon the integrity of the blood for nourishment, forming from it their individual patterns of composition, and renewal. Too few minerals in the food, insufficient vitamins, the wrong type of food, and faulty assimilation, these factors impoverish the blood and subsequently the fibres of muscles, the membranes of bones, and the articulations of joints. The electro-magnetic quality inherent in body tissues attracts those forms of nourishment necessary for its health, generally by means of the blood and lymph.

As well, the pattern-forms of all tissue are responsive to

[1] So far as is known to me, the British Biochemic Association are the only laboratories in this country who prepare specific compound prescriptions of these nutrients for the various conditions of these diseases.

nervous and emotional stimuli, both from within the body and outside it. The stimulus of anxiety causes tensed muscles, which if continuous prevents the full nourishment of these tissues, and in turn the adequate dispersal of the waste products through the somewhat restricted circulation. If persistent, the result is either an inflammatory or a toxic condition: this may take the form of rheumatism.

Qualities such as confidence and contentment bring relaxation of mind and of muscular tissues.

The use of the body beyond fatigue point brings undue wear and tear on those joints and tissues taking the stress of weight or friction, resulting first in inflammation, followed by degeneration of the articulations within the joint, which is a secondary process.

Nutritional deficiency is considered a contributing cause in some rheumatic and arthritic conditions. The deficiency suggested is one of keeping the body's calcium organized, its proper laying down in the tissues and being in solution in the blood and digestive juices. And for the promotion of a correct calcium balance, sufficient intake of vitamin D is the main nutritional key. (See also calcium-phosphorus absorption, p. 60.)

Apparently calcium can be organized all through life, and this point should be of interest to many sufferers whose calcium is out of balance.

Foods which are rich in potassium and sodium should also be included daily in the diet of those with rheumatism or arthritis, since these salts promote the correct fluidity of the cells and intercellular spaces of body tissues. A minute amount of iodine is another essential requirement, particularly where there is some disturbance in glandular function, which is often present in the oxygen-deficient type of rheumatism.

Three Food Dangers

There are three diet factors which need watching. The first is salt, the second is sugar, and the third the condition of the bowel.

The crude salt generally used in cooking, preserving, and at table is often taken in excess, and has been considered responsible by authoritative opinion for upsetting the body's sodium-potassium balance. Potassium acts as a *stabilizer* of the minerals and trace elements contained in healthy blood and tissues. Potassium is an inorganic chemical element of a compound nature and it is believed that crude salt displaces the values of its particles in relation to cell tissue, and is probably responsible for a number of serious diseases.

Little sugar is advisable for rheumatic sufferers, particularly those of the oxygen-deficient type. Sugar robs the body of its oxygen which it requires for its combustion in the tissues. Tea and coffee might well be taken without sugar, while honey and the dried fruits are advocated as better forms of sweetening where these can be used.

A healthy bowel promotes adequate vitamin and mineral absorption by the tissues. Where the natural secretions of the bowel and its own peristaltic action is insufficient to effect natural evacuations without additional stimulus, it is probable that the diet being followed is incorrect. The suggested menus should be tried for quite a period in an effort to establish a healthy condition.

Food and Menus for use in Rheumatism and Arthritis

Therefore, the meals of those who suffer with rheumatism or arthritis need specially to include foods which provide sufficient calcium and assimilable iron, and are a good source of iodine, potassium, sodium, vitamin D and its associated vitamins A and C, together with the intake needed of vitamin B.

Of course, all these constituents will not necessarily be found in one or two foods, but a good variety of the right foods should provide these nutritional essentials.

Suggested menus for a week follow, which are designed to provide these factors, suitably mixed, and attractive to personal needs. These meals will be found suitable for lacto-vegetarians, and those who eat flesh foods.

A higher intake of dairy foods is generally advised and a correspondingly low one of flesh food.

These menus cover general needs. They will not necessarily suit everyone, and may have to be adapted to suit individual requirements. Quantities are not given, leaving freedom in this matter; but the general scheme should be followed reasonably closely.

Menus for a Week

BREAKFASTS

Dandelion Coffee[1] or Orange Juice or Tea, of approximately only three minutes' standing. Darjeeling Orange Pekoe (a large-leaf, hill-grown tea), or Kenum China tea, or Matte tea, is suggested.

Four days a week

Orange jelly, using the juice of oranges, and made with carragheen[1] or agar-agar,[1] served with one tablespoonful of a wheat-germ food[1]

or

Milk jelly, made and served as above

or

Jellied blackcurrants when in season, made and served as above.

Three days a week

Apple muesli with sliced raw, ripe apple, oats, and a few blanched almonds, Barbados sugar, the juice of half a fresh lemon, and top of the milk.

---

[1] These items are all easily purchasable from good grocers and health stores: they are attractive to the palate when correctly prepared.

Toast and butter if desired, using, preferably, 85 per cent
extraction flour.

The jelly and the muesli breakfast dishes can be served
alternatively during the days of the week and so avoid mere
repetition of the dish as a sweet course for later in the day
unless personal choice dictates. The constituents of a dish
may be similar (giving needed mineral or vitamin factors)
but its treatment in preparation always gives some variety.

MIDDAY MEAL

A salad lunch with cheese

Choose a comparatively lightly salted variety of cheese:
English Cheddar, Wensleydale, Caerphilly: if a light protein
cheese is needed, the Cottage cheese or St. Ivel are recommended. Cream cheeses are rich in fat and light in protein,
and these can be included for variety, with suitable adjustments
to the rest of the meal.

The salad should contain as often as the season permits –
dandelion leaves, cucumber (diced and to include the skin),
chives, watercress, tomatoes, celery, beetroot, lettuce, parsley.

The watercress, and the young dandelion leaves – torn
from the mid-rib – should be used almost daily and obtained
fresh that day. The other items can be used for variety during
the week and include as an addition peas, turnips, spring
onions, capers, nasturtiums, garlic.

A particularly good mixture, and to be recommended also
for flavour, consists of watercress, dandelion leaves, parsley,
chives, and Caerphilly cheese.

The dry flavour of Wensleydale cheese blends well with a
salad of celery, tomatoes or beetroot or cucumber, and the
watercress.

Dress the salad if desired with olive oil and lemon juice.

Include boiled jacket potatoes at this meal

or

bread and butter, using as near as possible an 85 per cent extraction flour.

The salad lunch can at all times be interchanged with the evening meal. These follow. In cold weather, salad meals should begin with celery, tomato, or watercress soup, or a hot drink made with a vitamin B extract, such as Yeastrel or Marmite.

MID-MORNING AND MID-AFTERNOON DRINKS

Dandelion coffee, made with half milk, *or* a vitamin B drink *or* Tea of the varieties used for breakfast.

(No afternoon tea meal should be taken, nor cake or biscuits: the drink only.)

THE EVENING, OR COOKED MEAL

MONDAY: Cauliflower cheese, carrots, peas: apple crumble.

TUESDAY: Grilled or baked fish – fresh herring or white fish, with tomatoes and watercress and choice of vegetables

or

Sprouts and carrots with a nut dish

or

Spring greens, peas, and *Oeufs à la Normandie*.

(In this dish the eggs are poached and served with a little cream or cream cheese, which preferably should be added to the eggs during the last minute of cooking.)

Sweet of apple and orange salad with cream.

WEDNESDAY: Macédoine of carrots, celery, peas, turnips, potato, and grated cheese, *or* egg and mushroom pie.
Sweet of wheat germ preparation and raisins, with cream or the top of the milk.

THURSDAY: Soufflé, with kale, *or* cabbage, *or* young greens, and boiled or roast potatoes.
Sweet of rose apple tart.

FRIDAY: Omelette, *or* baked or grilled white fish, *or* tinned salmon.
French or runner beans, *or* green peas, potatoes.
Sweet of apple and sultana salad and cream *or* fresh fruits.

SATURDAY: Baked egg, onion and cheese dish with potatoes and watercress.
Sweet of orange jelly.

SUNDAY: Chicken *or* bucked egg[1] *or* roast lamb.
Sprouts *or* sprouting broccoli *or* garden peas, and roast or boiled jacket potatoes.
Sweet of fruit salad.

In many cases the Sunday cooked meal will be taken midday, and a late tea meal will follow in the early evening. Here bread and butter should be served with a green salad of dandelion leaves, celery, watercress, cress, chives, according to season, *or* sandwiches of the same, or of watercress and honey. Good home-made cakes, without sugar icing can also be served.

EVENING DRINKS

China tea, *or* dandelion coffee, *or* a vitamin B drink with milk, *or* a herb tea with honey, *or* Russian tea with lemon.

[1] In this dish a poached egg has the addition of a strip of plain cheese laid across the yolk and a sprinkling of dried or fresh herbs.

WINES

Sherry is considered unsuitable. It is a "plastered" wine, which means that at one stage of its production Calcium Sulphate is sprinkled on the grapes. This procedure has great antiquity. Its chemical effect is to produce an insoluble calcium in the wine, which later "falls out", clarifying the wine but taking the phosphates with it, and increasing the free acidity of the wine.

The free acidity and lack of phosphates may prove unkind to rheumatic sufferers.

A Marsala is suggested instead, *or* one of the liqueurs which includes herbs and fruits in its mixture,[1] *or* a good home-made wine, such as dandelion or elderberry.

How to make the Watercress Soup

Details were published in *The Listener*, several years ago. Boil a pound of potatoes in just enough water to cover them, and add half-way through a bunch of well-washed watercress. When the potatoes are done, rub all through a sieve, and season very lightly. It can be enriched just before serving with a little cream, or top of the milk, but part of its attraction is its simplicity of flavour.

[1] Curaçao, Chartreuse, Benedictine.